A SENSE OF HISTORY

The Roman Empire

JAMES MASON

ANGELA LEONARD
Assessment Consultant

Ashley
Dowling

LONGMAN

Acknowledgement

We are grateful to the following for permission to reproduce photographs:
Ancient Art and Architecture Collection/© Ronald Sheridan, pages 19 *right* 24 *top*, 30 *top*, 32 *top*, 38, 45 *bottom left*, 46 *top left*, 46 *bottom right*, 47 *bottom*, 62 *left*, 62 *right*, 86, 91; Ashmolean Museum, page 40; Barnaby's Picture Library, pages 35 *left*, 110 *right*; Bridgeman Art Library, pages 50 *top* (New York Historical Society), 97, 108, 110 *left*; British Film Institute, page 50 *bottom*, British Museum, pages 8, 11 *bottom left*, 11 *bottom right*, 51; Cambridge University Library, page 70; Centre Camille Jullian, page 60; Peter Clayton, page 15 *middle right*; Colchester Museum, page 69; Corbridge Roman Museum, page 36 *bottom left*; E M Dixon, pages 12, 25 *top*, 27 *centre left*, 30 *bottom*, 45 *top left*, 45 *top right*, 46 *top right*, 71, 74, 84, 85 *top*, 89, 91, 103 *top left*; © 1991 Les Editions Albert Renée/Goscinny-Underzo, page 111 *bottom*; Elsevier Archive, Amsterdam, page 35 *top right*; Mary Evans Picture Library, pages 96, 98 *top*; Werner Forman Archive, pages 19 *left*, 28 *top and bottom*, 105; Grosvenor Museum, Chester, page 27 *bottom*, Sonia Halliday, pages 45 *bottom right*, 47 *top left*, 47 *top centre*, 72; Robert Harding Picture Library, page 4; John Hawkins, pages 26, 109 *top*; Andre Held, page 87; Hirmer Verlag, pages 94 *left and right*; © Michael Holford, 15 *middle left*, 98 *bottom*, 103 *top right*; Judges Ltd, Hastings, page 29; Kingston upon Hull City Museum and Art Gallery, Transport and Archeology Museum, page 13; Magnum/Erich Lessing, page 74; Mansell Collection, pages 10 *right*, 11 *top*, 37 *top*, 42, 48, 49; Museo Capitolini, Rome, pages 15 *bottom left and bottom right*; Museo Pio Clementino, Rome, page 7; Museum of London, page 85 *bottom*; Museum of Wales, page 33; Naples Museum (Leonard von Matt), pages 34, 43, 44 *left*; National Museum of Wales, page 14, Photographie Giraudon, page 66; Pubbli Aerfoto, Milan, page 21; Royal Air Force, page 109 *centre*; Rex Features, page 107; Rheinisches Landmuseum, Trier, 37 *bottom*; Scala, pages 6, 22 *top*, 22 *top and bottom*, 23 *top left*, 24 *bottom middle*, 25 *bottom*, 44 *right*, 46 *bottom left*, 47 *top right*, 73, 109 *right*; Science Photo Library, page 17; Edwin Smith, page 23 *top right*, 24 *bottom right*, 79; Spectrum (Dallas and John Heaton), page 111 *top*; Tyne and Wear Museum, page 36 *top*; Roger Viollet, page 24 *bottom left*; Roger Wood, pages 31, 32 *bottom*, 59, 83.

We are unable to trace the following copyright holder and would be grateful for information that would enable us to do so: page 10 *left*.

Cover: Mosaic of Spring. Photo: © Michael Holford

Longman Group UK Limited
*Longman House, Burnt Mill, Harlow, Essex, CM20 2JE, England
and Associated Companies throughout the World*

© Longman Group UK Limited 1991

First published 1991
ISBN 0 582 20736 3

Typset in Monotype Lasercomp 12/14pt Photina
Printed in Great Britain by Butler & Tanner Limited, Frome

*The publisher's policy is to use paper manufactured
from sustainable forests*

Designed by Michael Harris
Illustrated by Oxford Illustrators Limited

Contents

1
A Roman Triumph

The Roman Empire

SOURCE 1

A modern photograph of the city of Rome.

Today thousands of tourists travel to Rome every year to see the remains of the buildings that stood there in ancient times.

Rome (source 1) is the capital city of Italy. About 4 million people live there. They speak Italian and call themselves Italians. 2,000 years ago the people who lived where Italy is today spoke Latin and called themselves Romans. The country of Italy did not exist.

2,000 years ago only 1 million people lived in Rome, yet the Romans ruled a vast **empire**. Their armies conquered lands that stretched from the Atlantic Ocean in the west to the River Euphrates in the east, and from Hadrian's Wall in the north to the edge of the Sahara Desert in the south.

The Roman Empire (source 2) was about 4,300 km long from west to east, and 3,200 km wide. You can see that it brought together and ruled over different peoples who spoke different languages and lived by different customs.

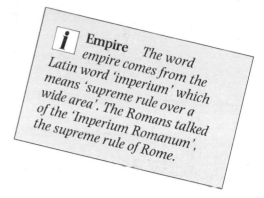

i **Empire** The word empire comes from the Latin word 'imperium' which means 'supreme rule over a wide area'. The Romans talked of the 'Imperium Romanum', the supreme rule of Rome.

SOURCE 2

The Roman Empire in AD 117 when it was at its largest. This map also shows you today's countries with their modern names. These countries did not exist in AD 117. The Romans divided the Empire into areas called provinces. You can see these in source 5 in Part 5.

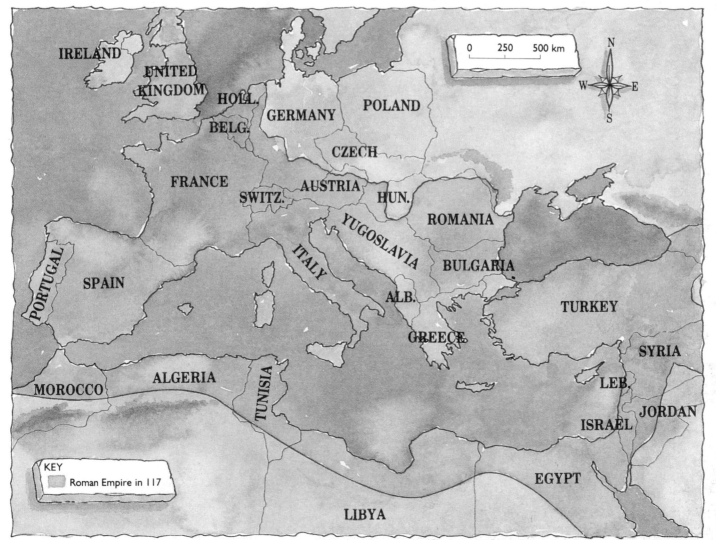

SOURCE 3

A model of the ancient city of Rome. Archaeologists built this using the clues provided by the remains of old buildings and the writings and pictures of the Romans themselves.

The Romans must have been skilled builders to create a city as splendid as the one in source 3 and they must have been good soldiers to conquer so large an empire. That much is obvious. But what were the Romans really like as a people? How did they live and what did they believe in? How did they come to rule such a big empire? And, if they were so clever, why didn't it last for ever? Does the fact that it did exist affect us today? These are some of the questions this book will help you to answer.

To start with you are going to find out a bit more about the Romans and their empire by visiting the city of Rome on a day when the Romans were celebrating the conquest of yet another land and its people.

The day was in the year AD 44. The land was Britain.

The conquest of Britain

Invasion

In the summer of the year AD 43 a messenger arrived with news for Emperor Claudius, the ruler of the Empire, from Plautius, the general in command of the army invading Britain.

Plautius said he was camped about 80 km away from the British stronghold at Camulodunum (modern Colchester). It was time for Claudius to go to Britain to lead his army in the final attack.

Claudius set out for Britain at once. As soon as he arrived he inspected the army and then led it against Camulodunum. When the town fell he entered it in a grand procession, which included elephants specially taken there for the occasion. Then he received the surrender of ten British kings and one queen in a solemn ceremony in front of his troops.

SOURCE 4

Soldiers on board a Roman ship. The crocodile tells us this ship was stationed in Egypt, but Claudius would probably have travelled to Britain in one like it.

When Claudius left to return to Rome, he had been in Britain for only sixteen days. All this was part of a careful plan. Plautius was a good general. He had no need of Claudius's help. But Claudius wanted to be seen to lead an army to victory.

Claudius was a clever man, very interested in Roman history, but he had never been a soldier. As a child he had an illness which meant he stammered and could not walk properly on his right leg which he dragged behind him. People often laughed at him and called him stupid. When he became Emperor, at the age of fifty-one, Claudius needed to prove himself.

The Romans had been interested in adding Britain to the Empire ever since Julius Caesar had twice invaded the island and left again in 55 and 54 BC. The previous emperor, Caligula, had prepared an expedition in AD 40 only to cancel it at the last moment. Claudius invaded Britain because he knew a successful expedition would be a certain way to impress both the Roman people and the Roman army.

He also knew they would be impressed by his daring because the Romans thought Britain stood on the edge of the world (see source 5) in a wild and dangerous sea which they called Oceanus. Julius Caesar's soldiers had been frightened to set out on this voyage into the unknown and Claudius's at first actually refused to board the ships.

> **i** **Ptolemy**   whose Latin name was Claudius Ptolemaeus, was part Greek and part Egyptian. He lived in Alexandria and was famous as a mathematician, geographer and astronomer. He wrote a book called Geography which was used until the sixteenth century.

SOURCE 5

A map of the world drawn by **Ptolemy** of Alexandria in the second century AD. This copy of the original map (which is now lost) was made in Italy in about 1470. Find Britain and Ireland at the top left.

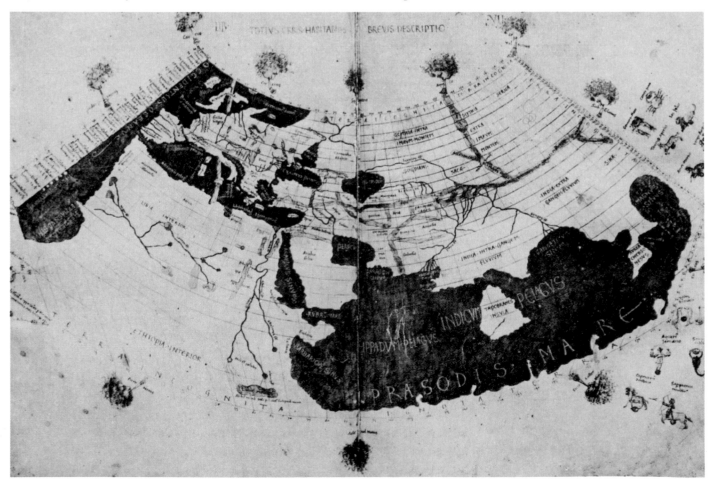

i **Beak** *The part of a ship that stuck out over its bows or front end.*

i **Suetonius** Suetonius was probably born in AD 69. He trained as a lawyer and became chief secretary to the Emperor Hadrian (AD 117–38). The Twelve Caesars tells of the lives of Julius Caesar and the first eleven Roman emperors. He consulted official government papers and talked to people who remembered some of the events.

When he got back to Rome, Claudius made sure that everyone knew what he had done:

SOURCE 6

*The emblems of Claudius's victory included the naval crown – ornamented with the **beaks** of ships and representing the crossing and conquest, so to speak, of the Ocean – which he set on the Palace gable [edge of the roof] beside a civic crown of oak-leaves.*

Suetonius, *The Twelve Caesars*, written early second century AD

Poems were written to celebrate his victories. These are lines from some of them:

SOURCE 7

Britain set apart in a vast and boundless ocean, surrounded by inaccessible shores.

She [Britain] surrendered as soon as she saw you, Caesar [Claudius].

What were once two separate worlds, are now joined in one.

activity

1 Look at source 7.
a What evidence is there that the Romans thought (i) Britain was in a remote and separate part of the world, (ii) the Ocean was wild and dangerous, and (iii) Claudius had an easy victory?
b Do you think the poems tell us what was true or only what Claudius wanted the Romans to believe? Explain your reasons.
2 Make a list of the reasons why you think Claudius put up the naval crown (source 6).

The news reaches Rome

When the news of his victory reached Rome the members of the chief council, called the Senate, immediately voted to give Claudius the title 'Brittanicus' (so now he was known as 'Claudius of Britain').

They also decided to hold a festival every year to commemorate the event and they ordered two arches, called 'Triumphal Arches', to be built – one in Rome and one in Gaul on the coast where the army set sail for Britain. Above all, they gave Claudius permission to hold a celebration called a 'triumph'.

It was the ambition of every Roman general to hold a triumph, which meant riding in procession through the streets of Rome being applauded by the people. Claudius's was the first triumph to be awarded to a reigning emperor for over seventy years.

Claudius's triumph

It took several days to prepare Rome for the triumph. Wooden scaffolding for spectators had to be put up in the streets and open spaces where the procession was to pass. The temples had to be opened and hung with flowers.

Early on the day itself people started to line the route while the procession formed – probably on the Campus Martius, Rome's ancient parade ground. By the time it was ready to set off, officers with staves were holding back the crowds which threatened to spill onto the route.

Claudius himself wore a wreath of bay leaves on his head and a silk robe dyed purple. He rode in a special triumphal car (source 8) escorted by the Emperor's personal troops, the Praetorian Guard (source 9).

Behind Claudius rode his wife, Messalina, in her own carriage, and behind her, also in purple robes, walked the other generals whose service in Britain had won them the honour of a triumph.

As well as the soldiers chosen to march in the procession, there were hundreds of Britons, captured in the fighting, who were now displayed to the crowds of curious Romans. Some of them were made to carry the booty taken from them by the Roman soldiers and there were cart-loads of British weapons and armour (source 11).

SOURCE 8

The Emperor Septimius Severus riding in his triumphal car. From the Arch of Severus in Leptis Magna – his native city in north Africa.

SOURCE 9

Soldiers of the Praetorian Guard.

SOURCE 10

The seven-branched candlestick from the Temple of Jerusalem being carried by Jewish captives in the triumph of Titus in AD 71. Find the placards carried to tell the crowds about each exhibit. Claudius's British captives would have been made to carry booty in the same way. From the Arch of Titus in Rome.

SOURCE 11

The bronze face of a wooden shield belonging to a wealthy Briton, found in the River Thames at Battersea. This was probably a ceremonial shield rather than one used for fighting.

SOURCE 12

A torque, or neck-ring, worn by wealthy British men and women, especially warriors. This one was found in Norfolk and may have belonged to the ruling family of the local tribe, the Iceni. Jewellery like this would have been included in the booty of Claudius's troops.

We do not know much about Claudius's triumph, but many triumphs included floats, or travelling stages, showing scenes from the war like the ones described by the writer Josephus who watched a triumph in AD 71:

SOURCE 13

Many of them were three or even four storeys high . . . and all were framed in . . . ivory and gold . . . Here was to be seen a smiling countryside laid waste, here whole formations of the enemy put to the sword . . . walls of enormous size thrown down by **siege-engines**, *great strongholds stormed . . .*

Josephus, *The Jewish War*, completed in AD 75

At last the procession reached the Temple of Jupiter, the Romans' chief god and protector of the Empire. Every triumphal procession ended here with the general giving thanks to Jupiter for his victory.

Claudius knelt at the bottom of the steps leading up to the temple and then painfully went up them on his knees, supported on either side by his sons-in-law. At the top, outside the temple, he performed the traditional sacrifices to the god (source 14).

> **i** **Siege-engine** A siege happens when an army tries to capture a town or castle by surrounding it so as to cut it off from the outside world and especially from its food supplies. Siege-engines were machines such as catapults and battering rams which were used to break down the walls of a city under siege.

SOURCE 14

A sacrifice. The Romans killed animals and offered their bodies to their gods to please them and keep them on their side. The Romans believed each sacrifice had to be carried out in a particular way. Any mistake made the offering useless.

The triumphal celebrations ended with a festival:

SOURCE 15

Claudius had announced as many horse-races as could take place in a day, yet there were not more than ten of them. For between the different races bears were slain, athletes contested, and boys from Asia performed the **Pyrrhic dance** *... Another festival ... was given by artists of the stage.*

Cassius Dio, *Roman History*, completed early third century AD

> **i** **Pyrrhic dance** The war-dance of the ancient Greeks. The dancers wore armour and went through the actual movements of fighting accompanied by music.

activity

1 Look at sources 8 and 10.
a Make a list of all the information each one gives you about a Roman triumph.
b The Arch of Titus (source 10) was built about 40 years after Claudius's triumph and the Arch of Septimius Severus (source 8) about 160 years after that. How useful do you think these sources are for telling us about Claudius's triumph?
2 Look at sources 11 and 12. If you were a Roman watching the procession what impression of Britain and the British would you get from objects like these?
3 Look at sources 16 and 3.
a Find the Circus Maximus in source 3.
b How would source 16 have been useful to the archaeologists building the model of Rome (source 3)?

SOURCE 16

This British mosaic shows charioteers driving their teams of horses in a race in an arena, like Rome's Circus Maximus. There were four teams named Red, White, Blue and Green after their colours. Fights often broke out among their fans.
Find:
● the triple turning posts

Caratacus in Rome

SOURCE 17

A coin of
Caratacus.

i Tacitus Cornelius Tacitus was born about AD 56. He was a member of the Senate and became governor of the province of western Anatolia before his death sometime after 117. He said his aim as a historian was to write down both the good and the evil actions of people in the past so that those who lived later could judge them. The Annals of Imperial Rome told the story of the Roman emperors from the death of Augustus (AD 14) to the death of Nero (AD 68).

When Claudius held his triumph in AD 44 the Romans thought they had done enough to control the British. But one king in particular, Caratacus, held out against them for seven more years. At last, in AD 51, he was defeated and captured in central Wales.

Claudius used the surrender of Caratacus to summon the people of Rome to yet another spectacular ceremony. The Praetorian Guard were drawn up on the parade ground in front of their barracks and Claudius and his wife sat on raised platforms to watch a march past of soldiers and captives.

SOURCE 18

As the king's [Caratacus's] followers marched along, their decorations and torques, and the spoils they had won in wars against other British tribes were displayed. Then came Caratacus's brothers, his wife and daughter, finally the king himself . . .

Tacitus, *The Annals of Imperial Rome*, completed early second century AD

It was the Roman custom to execute captured leaders; but Claudius allowed Caratacus make a speech. According to Tacitus he told the Romans he could have entered their city as a friend and powerful ally rather than as a captive:

SOURCE 19

I possessed horses, men, arms and wealth. Is it surprising if I have been unwilling to give these up? For if it is your desire to rule over the whole world, does it follow that all men should readily accept slavery? . . . If you put me to death, I shall be forgotten. But if you preserve my life, I shall be an everlasting witness to your clemency [mercy].

Tacitus, *The Annals of Imperial Rome*, completed early second century AD

Claudius replied by granting a pardon to Caratacus and his family. It is thought they then lived on in Rome as honoured guests.

activity

1 Look at source 19. The Roman people thought highly of leaders who showed 'clemency', or mercy, to others. How does that help to explain why Claudius allowed Caratacus to make his speech?
2 The Roman people also admired leaders who showed 'piety', that is respect for and obedience to the gods. Look at page 12. How did Claudius manage to show his piety during his triumph?

The Arch of Claudius

In AD 52, the builders finished Claudius's Triumphal Arch in Rome. It has long since fallen down, though other Triumphal Arches – such as the Arch of Titus (source 20) – still stand.

Only three pieces of evidence have come to light which we can use as clues to how it may have looked. There is a coin of Claudius's time (source 21), there is a piece of a relief, or sculpture, from the arch (source 22), and there is part of the inscription (writing carved in stone) which told of Claudius and what he had done (source 23).

SOURCE 20

The Arch of Titus. Claudius's Arch would have looked something like this.

SOURCE 21

A coin showing a statue of Claudius on horseback between piles of booty on top of his Triumphal Arch.

SOURCE 23

Part of the inscription from the Arch of Claudius.

SOURCE 22

A relief from the Arch of Claudius, found in 1925.

assignments

I What kind of people were the Romans according to the sources and information in Part I?
a Make a list of words which you think describe them best (for example, warlike, proud).
b Write a few sentences to explain why you have chosen each word.
c Choose the two characteristics (two words from your list) of the Romans that you least admire so far and the two you most admire. Say why you have chosen each one.
d Form a small group and share your opinions with the others in your group. Decide on which points you agree and on which you disagree.

2 What have you found out so far from the information and sources in Part I about the job of being Roman Emperor?
a Describe the various different tasks that the Emperor had to carry out.
b Describe the personal qualities that you think the Emperor needed to have.
c Which of these qualities did Claudius have and which did he not have?

3 Historians try to work out what happened in the past using the clues they find in the source material. Sometimes the same source can be used to support different interpretations of what happened. For instance, Roman writers do not make it clear whether or not Claudius actually led his army in a battle against the British. Many modern historians think he did; but some think all he did was to accept the surrender of the British kings. One source tells us how Claudius celebrated his victory in Britain every year as the Senate had suggested:

SOURCE 24

He ... displayed the capture and plunder of a British town, and the surrender of the British kings, over which he presided in his purple campaigning cloak.

Suetonius, *The Twelve Caesars*, written early second century AD

a How could you use this source to show:
(i) Claudius did take part in a battle;
(ii) he did not?
b Why do you think it is so hard to be sure whether he did or not, even though he was awarded a triumph?

4 The Romans lining the streets to watch Claudius's triumph saw it from a completely different point of view to the Britons in the procession.
a Imagine you are a Roman who watched the triumph. Write a letter to a friend who missed it describing what you saw and felt that day.
b Imagine you are a British captive who was paraded in the triumph. Afterwards you talk to your fellow captives about your experiences that day and what you saw and felt. Write the conversation you might have had.

2

Roman Cities

The lost cities

Disaster

In the year AD 79 the two Roman towns of Pompeii and Herculaneum disappeared in the course of just a few hours. They both stood to the south of Mount Vesuvius, near the modern town of Naples, in Italy.

Vesuvius was a volcano and the people of Pompeii knew there was a danger because the city had been badly damaged by an earthquake seventeen years before. But no one was prepared for what happened on 24 August AD 79.

Early that morning Vesuvius gave out a deafening crack and the ground for miles around shook violently. One moment the top of the mountain was slightly curved like the top of a loaf of bread, the next it was split open and jagged.

A mixture of smoke, flames, burning mud – called lava – and red hot stones roared up into the darkened sky. The stones shot for miles like rockets. Wherever they landed they started fires.

Lava poured down the mountain crushing houses, sweeping away trees and rolling on towards the seashore. There the waves boiled and foamed as the lava pushed them back across the sand.

SOURCE 1

A volcano erupting in Hawaii in 1983.

SOURCE 2

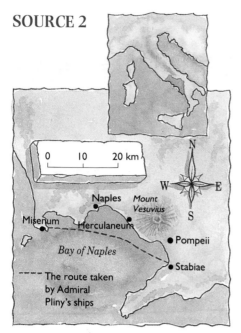

The Bay of Naples and the towns near Vesuvius.

A survivor remembers

That summer a young Roman called Caius Pliny was staying about fifteen miles away in the port of Misenum where his uncle, Admiral Pliny, commanded a fleet of warships. Twenty-five years later he wrote to his friend, the historian Cornelius Tacitus, telling him what he remembered.

First he told how his uncle sailed across the bay to try to rescue people trapped between Vesuvius and the sea. He landed safely but, with the wind against him, he could not set sail again. So he went to rest in a friend's house.

The house started to collapse so Admiral Pliny went back to the beach to see if it was possible to sail again; but the waves were too dangerous. Then the heat and smell of approaching lava forced everyone to move:

SOURCE 3

My uncle stood leaning on two slaves and then suddenly collapsed, I imagine because the dense fumes choked his breathing by blocking his windpipe which was . . . weak and narrow. When daylight returned . . . two days later, his body was found . . . uninjured, still fully clothed and looking more like sleep than death.

Pliny, *Letter to Tacitus*, written about 104

Meanwhile Caius Pliny and his mother were still at Misenum. In the morning they decided to leave:

SOURCE 4

Ashes were already falling . . . I looked round: a dense black cloud was coming up behind us, spreading over the earth like a flood.

Pliny, *Letter to Tacitus*, written about 104

They left the road to avoid being trampled by the crowd and sat down in a field. Suddenly it went completely dark as if someone had put out the lamp in a closed room:

SOURCE 5

Many prayed for the help of the gods, but still more imagined there were no gods left . . . Ashes began to fall . . . in heavy showers. We rose from time to time and shook them off, otherwise we would have been buried and crushed beneath their weight.

Pliny, *Letter to Tacitus*, written about 104

At last the cloud began to roll away and they saw a changed world with everything buried deep in ashes like snowdrifts. They waded through them back to Misenum and started to clear up the house, waiting for news of the admiral.

The mysterious holes

When Vesuvius erupted, Pompeii and Herculaneum disappeared under ashes and mud for over 1,500 years. Grass grew over the sites. People forgot they had ever been there.

Later a legend grew up. People said that somewhere beneath the ground there lay a fabulously wealthy city. No one knew its name. They simply called it 'La Citta' – 'The City'. In 1748 treasure hunters started to search for it and soon they came across the remains of the two towns.

In 1860 an archaeologist called Fiorelli, who was in charge of the digging at Pompeii, found mysterious holes in the solidified ashes. He worked out that the ashes had covered the bodies of people trying to escape and had then hardened. Later the bodies rotted away leaving the holes.

Fiorelli ordered a hole to be filled with liquid plaster. As it hardened it took on the shape of a body. Then he cut carefully round it to reveal the plaster cast.

Archaeologists still use this method today. By looking at the plaster casts they can work out the details of the last moments in the lives of the people who died.

SOURCE 6

A woman who appears to have died in the street.

SOURCE 7

This dog was chained outside a house. He tried to climb up the pile of ashes as they fell on him. Then the chain reached full stretch and he died fighting to get free.

City life

At the moment when ash and lava engulfed the buildings and the people of Pompeii and Herculaneum, time stopped in the two cities. Now, thanks to the work of archaeologists, you can walk around the ruins and see the remains of the cities much as they were on 24 August AD 79.

Of course, there were hundreds of other cities in the Empire, and archaelogists have found things out about the Romans from them too. Now you are going to look at some of the buildings and objects which can tell us about life in a Roman city and the Romans' skills as builders and craftspeople.

Planning a city

The Romans thought cities were important so they planned them very carefully. But before you look at their ideas, think about your own town. A lot of people live in a modern town or city. What do they need to make life pleasant?

When the Romans built a new city or added to an old one, they planned it so that the streets went in straight lines with the buildings in the square blocks between them. They borrowed this idea from the Greeks.

Many of the blocks were for houses, but some were for the buildings the Romans thought every town should have. You can see these labelled on the plan (source 8).

---

activity

Work in pairs. You are in charge of planning a new town. Here are some of the things you could have in it to make life pleasant: cinema; swimming pool; public lavatories; sports hall; theatre; bingo hall; market; park; shopping precinct; health centre.
1 Number these 1 to 10 in the order of importance you think they have. Make 1 the most important.
2 What other important things have been left out? Make a list of them and decide where they come in your order of importance.
3 Compare your decisions with another pair and discuss them.

SOURCE 8

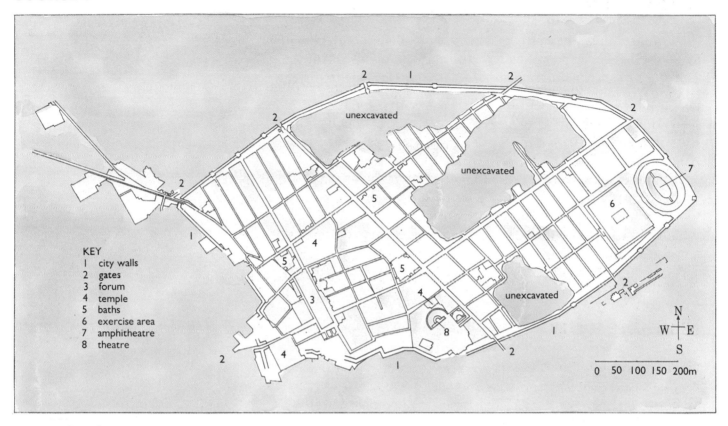

KEY
1 city walls
2 gates
3 forum
4 temple
5 baths
6 exercise area
7 amphitheatre
8 theatre

0 50 100 150 200m

A street plan of Pompeii.

SOURCE 9

Pompeii from the air. Compare this to the plan (source 8). Which buildings can you find?

Streets and shops

The Romans made their streets with stone and built high pavements on each side to keep people clear of the carts going up and down. They built in special crossing stones, with gaps for carts to drive through, for when the road was wet and muddy.

Shops opened on to the pavements and houses lay behind the shops.

SOURCE 10

A road in Pompeii. Find the crossing stones.

SOURCE 11

A shop scene. Find the things for sale.

SOURCE 12

SOURCE 13

A loaf of bread from the bakery, preserved by the ashes.

The remains of a bakery that opened onto the street in Pompeii. Find:
● the oven. What is it made of? How has the opening been built?
● the round stones for grinding corn. The holes in the tops held wooden poles which were probably turned by donkeys.

Houses

Source 14 shows you the plan of a typical Roman house belonging to a fairly wealthy family. The rooms on each side of the entrance faced the street. Slaves usually lived there, though in Pompeii many owners turned them into shops or snack bars.

SOURCE 14

A plan of a single-storey town house in Pompeii. The unmarked rooms would have included living rooms, bedrooms, a study, a kitchen and a lavatory. Only very large houses had bathrooms. Most people had to use the public baths.

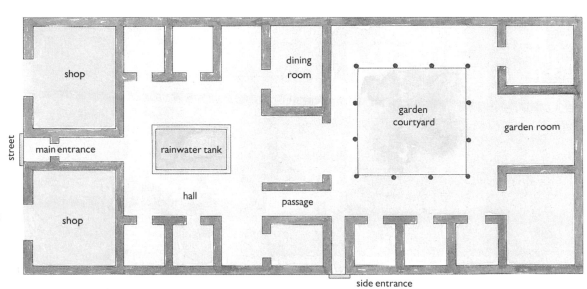

Inside, all the main rooms faced into a central hall (source 15) which had an opening overhead to let in air and light, and a tank set into the floor beneath to catch the rainwater. There were no windows. All the light had to come through the roof of the hall. Other rooms faced into the garden (source 16) which was surrounded by pillars and walkways.

activity

1 Look at sources 15, 16, 17 and 18. What does each one tell you about:
a life in a Roman town?
b the skills of Roman artists and craftspeople?

SOURCE 15

The hall of a house in Herculaneum.

SOURCE 16

The garden of a house in Pompeii.

SOURCE 17

A brass lamp-stand from Pompeii.

SOURCE 18

A glass bowl and ornament from Pompeii.

SOURCE 19

The ruins of apartment blocks in Ostia near Rome.

SOURCE 20

A model of an apartment block. Flats with five or six rooms stood on each side of a wide corridor on each storey. Find:
- the shops on the ground level
- the narrow entrance with steps to the floors above
- the balconies

Poorer people lived in flats in big apartment blocks (sources 19 and 20). These were not always very safe places to live in:

SOURCE 21

We're living in a city that's propped up with little more than matchsticks: and they're the only way the rent-man can keep his tenants from falling out, as he plasters over the gaps in the cracks and tells them not to worry . . . (even if the place is just about to fall around them!). It's wrong for people to have to live in fear of house-fires and buildings collapsing all the time.

Juvenal, *Satires*, written about the end of the first century AD

> **i** **Juvenal** *was a poet who lived from about AD 60 to about 136. He called his poems 'satires'. A satire is a piece of writing which shows up peoples' wrongdoings and weaknesses by making fun of them.*

activity

2a Make a list of all the differences between apartments (sources 19 and 20) and town houses (sources 14–16).
b Which is the most like a modern house? How is it the same? How is it different?
3a What does Juvenal (source 21) say is wrong with apartments in Rome?
b Who does he blame for this?

Water

The Romans believed that every city should have a water supply. They thought this was so important that their water engineers often tunnelled through mountains and built bridges across steep valleys so that an **aqueduct** could carry water from a river, lake or spring to one of their cities.

By the end of the first century AD nine aqueducts with a total length of 425 km delivered over 22 million gallons of water into Rome every twenty-four hours.

According to Admiral Pliny, who is known as the Elder Pliny:

> **i** **Aqueduct** A channel or pipeline for carrying water. The word comes from the Latin word 'aquae-ductus', meaning carrier (ductus) of water (aquae). Some Roman aqueducts were more than 80 km long.

SOURCE 22

One must rate all this as the most remarkable achievement anywhere in the world.

Elder Pliny, *Natural History*, written mid first century AD

SOURCE 23

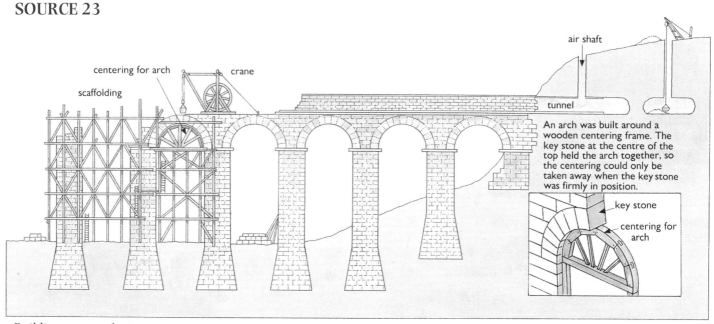

An arch was built around a wooden centering frame. The key stone at the centre of the top held the arch together, so the centering could only be taken away when the key stone was firmly in position.

Building an aqueduct.

SOURCE 24

The aqueduct at Segovia in Spain, built around the beginning of the second century AD.

SOURCE 25

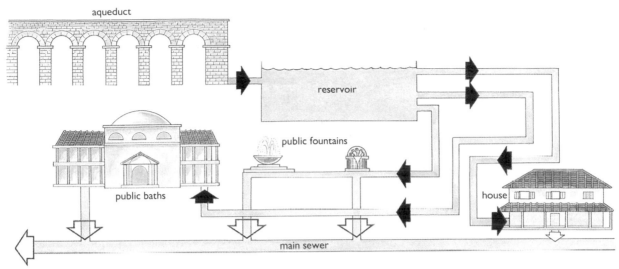

How water was sent from an aqueduct to where it was needed in the town. The pipes left the reservoir at three levels. So, if the water level inside fell, they were cut off one by one. Which was cut off first? Which last?

SOURCE 26

A public lavatory in Pompeii. Very few houses had bathrooms or lavatories so most people used the public ones like these. The Romans also built massive underground sewers to carry dirt and waste away from the cities.

SOURCE 28

Lead water pipes from Chester in Britain.

SOURCE 27

A street fountain in Pompeii. Most people throughout the Empire collected their water from fountains like this.

activity

1 Look at sources 23 and 24.
a How did the Romans design and build an aqueduct?
b The aqueduct was built in about 100. The photograph was taken in 1991. What does this tell you about the Romans as builders?
2 Look at source 22. Do you agree or disagree with the Elder Pliny? What are your reasons?
3 Look at sources 25–28. What do they tell you about
a Roman health;
b Roman technology?

The baths

The public baths were the social centre of every Roman city. They were a cross between a modern sauna and a Turkish bath. They had a courtyard for exercising and sometimes a swimming pool. Most Romans went there every day to get clean, keep fit and chat.

There were several rooms in the public baths. First you undressed in the changing room. Then you exercised in the courtyard and went to sit in a room heated with warm air. Then you went to a very hot one.

The hot air made you sweat so an attendant rubbed you over with olive oil and then scraped if off with a tool made of metal or ivory called a strigil. This cleansed the skin. After that you went back to the warm room to cool down and perhaps have a massage, before finishing off with a cold plunge in the pool.

SOURCE 29

The women's changing room at the baths of Herculaneum.
Find:
- the floor mosaic of sea creatures
- the shelf around the wall with the wooden compartments for clothes. Bathers took slaves with them to guard their clothes.

SOURCE 30

The men's hot room in the Forum Baths, Pompeii. This room and the women's hot room next to it were heated by hot air from a central furnace. The marble basin held water for the bathers to sponge themselves.

SOURCE 31

The under-floor heating system at Bath. Hot air from the furnace circulated under the floor and up channels built into the walls. Bathers had to wear wooden sandals because the floors were so hot.

The writer **Seneca** gives us a good idea of the hustle and bustle going on around the baths:

SOURCE 32

I have lodgings right over the public baths. So imagine the . . . sounds . . . the arresting of an occasional . . . pick pocket, the racket of the man who always likes to hear his own voice in the bathroom, or the enthusiast who plunges into the swimming tank with far too much noise and splashing . . . Imagine the hair-plucker with his penetrating, shrill voice . . . continually shouting and never holding his tongue except when he is plucking the armpits and making his victim yell instead. Then the cake-seller . . . the sausageman, the confectioner, and all the sellers of food calling out their wares . . .

Seneca, *Letters*, written about AD 50

i **Seneca** Seneca was born in Corduba, Spain, in about 4 BC. He became a philosopher, poet, dramatist and statesman. He was a famous speechmaker and was tutor and adviser to the Emperor Nero until AD 62 when he retired because he could no longer stand Nero's crimes. In 65 he was accused of plotting against the Emperor and committed suicide.

The amphitheatre

The Romans went to the amphitheatre to watch fights to the death between armed men, called gladiators, and between gladiators and wild animals. Pompeii's amphitheatre was the oldest in the Empire. It had been built in 80 BC, exactly 100 years before the amphitheatre in Rome, called the Colosseum, was opened.

The Romans set aside ninety-three days a year for games and shows. When the Colosseum was opened the fighting lasted for 100 days and over 1,000 gladiators and 9,000 animals died.

SOURCE 33

The amphitheatre in Pompeii.

SOURCE 34

A wall painting from Pompeii showing a riot in the amphitheatre in AD 59.

activity

1a What do sources 33 and 34 tell you about how the amphitheatre might have looked in AD 79?
b Make drawings of what you think it looked like inside and outside.

SOURCE 35

A **mosaic** showing gladiators fighting.

> **i** **Mosaics** The Romans were good at making pictures on walls and floors by sticking together very small pieces of stone or glass in patterns. These are called mosaics.

Seneca was one of the few people who attacked the Roman people's love of bloodshed. This is how he described a midday entertainment in the arena, when criminals were made to fight each other to the death with no armour to protect them:

SOURCE 36

Most people prefer this kind of thing to all other matches . . . The sword is not checked [stopped] by helmet or shield. What good is armour? What good is swordsmanship? All these things only put off death a little . . . can't you people see . . . that bad examples come back to haunt those who set them?

Seneca, *Moral Epistles*, mid first century AD

activity

2 Look at source 36.
a What reasons does Seneca give for people liking this kind of fight best?
b How can you tell that he disapproves of it?
3 Make a list of modern sports or entertainments that you think are cruel or have bad effects on those who watch them or take part. What bad effects do they have?

The theatre

Nearly every city in the Empire had a theatre for plays, dancing, miming and concerts. The shows were provided free, usually by a wealthy citizen who wanted to gain the favour of the townspeople.

SOURCE 37

A mosaic from Pompeii showing actors rehearsing a play. Find their masks.

SOURCE 38

The ruins of the theatre at Leptis Magna in north Africa.
Find:
- the empty semi-circle, called the 'orchestra'. Important people such as councillors and magistrates sat there
- the rows of stone seats for the other spectators
- the doors for the audience
- the stairs and gangways for them to reach their seats

The stage was on the low supports in front of the orchestra. It was wide and quite narrow. There were three doors for actors to enter and leave the stage and a storeroom and dressing rooms behind it.

The forum

SOURCE 39

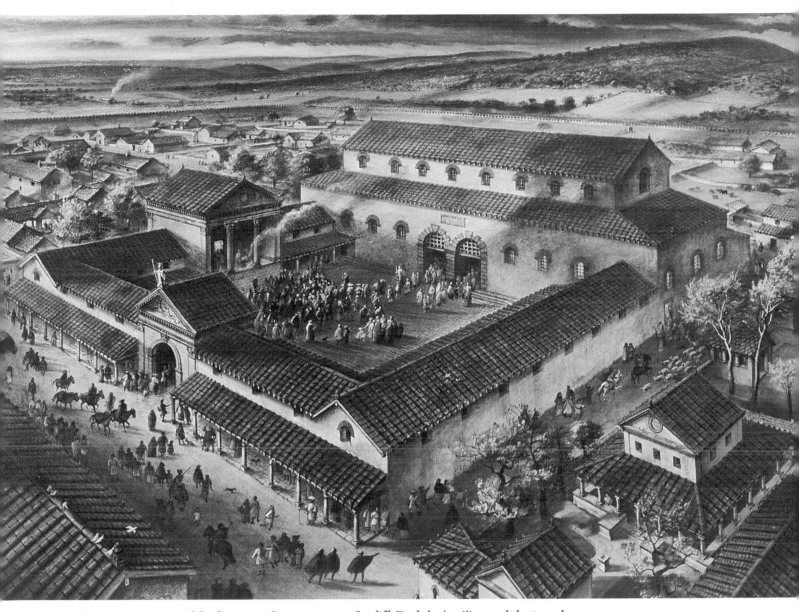

An artist's re-construction of the forum at Caerwent near Cardiff. Find the basilica and the temple.

The main square, or forum, was the centre of life in every Roman city. A large hall, called a basilica, stood on one side. The people who ran the town worked here. It was also the law courts and a large indoor assembly place.

On the other sides there were temples and covered areas where money lenders, tax gatherers and business people set up their stalls. There were shops there too, and a market in the middle.

People also met there to chat and discuss what was going on in the city. There was a platform where public criers stood to give out news and where politicians made speeches to try to win votes.

The town council

When archaeologists uncovered the remains of the forum in Pompeii, they found writings on the walls of the buildings – sometimes on posters, sometimes scratched or scribbled like graffiti. Here are some of the things they said:

SOURCE 40

'Vote for Brutus. He'll keep the taxes down.'

'Primius the laundryman wants Lucius Ceius to be mayor.'

'Vote for Cornelius and Albucius to be keepers of the market. We need men like them in the city.'

'The farmers want Cornelius to be mayor.'

'The thieves want you to vote for Vatia.'

'All the drunkards want Cerrisius to be mayor.'

Every year the citizens had to elect four officers, or magistrates, – two mayors, who acted as judges and organised voting for the elections, and two others who supervised the upkeep of the roads, market and public baths, and organised public games.

The idea of having two of each kind was that they could keep watch on each other so there was less chance that one of them would cheat the town or steal its money. Also it meant that they both had to agree in order for anything to be done. That meant that their plans were more likely to be sensible.

They also had to listen to the advice of the town council. No one elected the town council. Instead each magistrate automatically became a councillor once his year of office was over. Women could not be magistrates or councillors.

You could only become a councillor if you owned a certain amount of property. Most wealthy men wanted the honour of becoming councillors. Being on the council gave them the power to influence the running of the city's affairs. So they gave money for buildings or entertainments in the hope that the grateful citizens would elect them as magistrates.

These verses were written by the people of a city in Spain under a statue of one of their mayors:

SOURCE 42

In honour of Lucius Lucretius.
He was the town councillor, mayor and chief priest of the city.
He gave us a circus and beast show lasting four days.
He gave us chariot races free.
He gave all the citizens of our town a free banquet.

activity

1 What can you tell from source 40 about elections in Pompeii?

2a What do sources 41 and 42 show about the benefits of having wealthy people as city councillors?

b Do you think there were any disadvantages in having only wealthy men as councillors?

SOURCE 41

The people of Herculaneum put up this statue of Marcus Nonius Balbus to honour him for his gifts to the city. He was probably one of its richest citizens. He paid for the rebuilding of the town hall after an earthquake in AD 62 and for the building of public baths. He is wearing a woollen robe called a 'toga'.

assignments

1 Source 43 shows the ruins of the city of Timgad in Africa from the air. Source 44 is a view from the ground. Make a list of the things that you can see that tell you that this was a Roman city. Explain what each thing is and why it is evidence that the Romans built the town.

SOURCE 43

SOURCE 44

2 You have found out about Roman cities by using many different sources of evidence, mostly found by archaeologists.
a Find one example from Part 2 of each of these kinds of archaeological source: a building; a painting; writing; a mosaic; a household object. What other kinds of archaeological source have you used?
b What information about Roman cities can each of these different kinds of archaeological source give us?
c What sort of things survive for archaeologists to find and what sort of things do not?
d What information can archaeological sources <u>not</u> give us?

3 Make lists of the similarities and differences between Roman cities and modern cities. Think about (i) the way people lived, (ii) the facilities (eg. shops), and (iii) town organisation (eg. councils). Take <u>two</u> of these, one similarity and one difference, and describe them in as much detail as you can.

4a Make either a detailed model or a detailed drawing of one of the following:

- inside the baths at Pompeii at its busiest time
- the amphitheatre at Pompeii during a gladiatorial fight

Use the source material that you have already studied and any other information that you can find to make the model or picture as accurate as you can.
b Keep a list to show those things which you are sure about and those which you have to guess. If you are sure about something make a note of the source of your information. How reliable is your information in each case?

5 Use the sources and information in Part 2 and any other information you can find in libraries to give a short talk about the skills of Roman builders and engineers. Illustrate it with diagrams.

3

Roman People

Citizens and slaves

SOURCE 1

Regina's tombstone. She is
shown wearing an elegant
gown. Find:
- her jewel box and
  workbasket with wool
  in it
- the Latin writing
  underneath. Do you
  recognise any of the
  words?
- the writing at the bottom
  in Barates's native
  language

SOURCE 2

Barates's tombstone.

Barates was a flag bearer in the Roman army whose home was in
the city of Palmyra in the Syrian desert. He was posted to Britain
where he married a local girl from a British tribe called the
Catuvellauni. She died aged thirty. He died when he was sixty-eight.

We know all this from their tombstones. His was found at
Corbridge and hers at South Shields, both on Hadrian's Wall in
northern Britain (see page 70). The girl was called Regina which is
a Latin word meaning 'queen'. We do not know who chose this
name for her or when. Perhaps it was Barates himself.

Regina's tombstone tells us something more. The writing says
that Barates bought her as a slave and at some point he freed her,
probably when they got married.

When the Romans conquered new lands, they usually captured
some of their people to be slaves. As a result two sorts of people lived
in the Empire: the men and women who had been born free and
could call themselves citizens; and those who were slaves.

SOURCE 3

Slaves preparing dinner. The Romans ate their main meal in mid-afternoon. From a monument.

SOURCE 4

Slaves helping their mistress to do her hair. From a tomb.

Wherever people born of free parents lived, they could call themselves citizens of Rome. If they were men they had the right to vote for town councillors and to wear a long robe draped from the shoulders called a 'toga' (see source 41 on page 34).

Most well-off families owned slaves who did the cooking, shopping and household tasks and acted as servants. Wealthy landowners used slaves to work on their estates as labourers. Some educated slaves were owned by town councils and worked as clerks and officials. The Emperor owned slaves who did important jobs helping him to run the Empire.

But, no matter how important the work of a slave was, she or he had to obey or be punished, could be bought and sold as a piece of property and was unable to vote or hold office as councillor or magistrate.

Caius Pliny thought he treated his slaves quite well.

SOURCE 5

I am always ready to grant my slaves their freedom; and I allow those who remain unfree to make a sort of will . . . They give their . . . requests and I carry them out as if they were orders. They can leave their possessions to anyone they like so long as the slave who inherits them is actually living in the household; for the house provides a slave with a country and a sort of citizenship.

Pliny, *Letters*, written 103–7

But Pliny could be frightened of slaves too:

SOURCE 6

Larcius Masedo, a Senator, has fallen victim to his own slaves. Admittedly he was a proud and cruel master . . .

He was taking a bath when suddenly his slaves surrounded him. One seized him by the throat, while the others hit him in the face, chest and stomach. When they thought he was dead they threw him onto the hot floor to make certain . . .

There you see the dangers, outrages and insults to which we are exposed. No master can feel safe just because he is kind and considerate. It is their brutality which leads slaves to murder masters. Reason does not come into it.

Pliny, *Letters*, written 97–102

SOURCE 7

A baker from Pompeii and his wife who is shown holding a writing tablet and pen. Perhaps that means she kept the accounts for the shop.

Sometimes a master such as Barates might free a slave. In that case, the slave became a freedwoman or freedman. Source 7 shows a portrait of a freedman and his wife. He owned a bakery in Pompeii.

Freedmen could own property, but they were not full citizens. They could not vote, they were not allowed to wear the toga and they could not become town councillors. But their sons were citizens and could do all these things provided they had enough money.

Freedmen were often looked down upon by citizens:

SOURCE 8

I happened to be dining with a man . . . who . . . put the wine into tiny little flasks, divided into three categories. One lot was . . . for himself and for us, another for his lesser friends and the third for his and our freedmen.

My neighbour at table noticed this and asked me if I approved. I said I did not. 'So what do you do?' he asked. 'I serve the same to everyone, for when I invite guests it is for a meal, not to make class distinctions.' 'Even the freedmen?' 'Of course, for then they are my fellow-diners, not freedmen.'

Pliny, *Letters*, written 108–9

activity

I Look at source 5.
a List all the ways in which Pliny says he treated his slaves well.
b What other evidence is there that Pliny cared for his slaves?
2 Look at source 6.
a What criticisms does Pliny make of Masedo?
b What criticisms does he make of Masedo's slaves?
c If Pliny felt that Masedo was a cruel master, why did he disapprove of the slaves' actions?
d What evidence is there that Pliny was frightened by the story of Masedo?
e From the evidence of these sources what do you think Pliny felt about slaves?
3a How does source 8 show that Pliny treated his freedmen well?
b What evidence is there that other people did not treat their freedmen in this way?

Rich and poor

There was a great difference between the richest and poorest people in Rome. Caius Pliny became one of the richest. Today we would call him a millionaire. The Romans calculated their wealth in a unit of money called a 'sesterce'. Pliny was probably worth about 20,000,000 sesterces. As well as his house in Rome, he owned two large 'villas', or country houses (source 10), and plenty of farming land.

It is difficult to calculate what a sesterce would be worth in today's money but we know that the Emperors often gave hand-outs of six sesterces a day to the poorest people in Rome. So that was probably the least a person could manage to live on.

We know from the poet **Martial** that even citizens could be poor:

i Martial was born in Spain in about AD 40 and died about 104. He invented the 'epigram' which is a short poem with a clever point or twist at the end. For example: 'He who thinks Acerra reeks [smells strongly] of yesterday's wine is wrong: Acerra always drinks till dawn.'

SOURCE 9

What the poor have to put up with every day is a pot with a broken handle, a miserable fireplace without a fire, a beggar's rug, a rickety old camp-bed riddled with bed bugs, a toga that's too short and worn both day and night.

Martial, *Epigrams*, written late first century AD

SOURCE 10

A model of one of Pliny's villas. It was by the sea just south of Ostia, near Rome.

Some freedmen became very rich:

SOURCE 11

Look at Caius Caecidius Isidorus, the former slave of Caius. On the 27 January 8 BC he declared in his will that although he had suffered great losses during the Civil War, he was still able to leave for his heirs 4,116 slaves, 3,600 pairs of oxen, 257,000 head of cattle of other kinds and 60,000,000 sesterces in cash. And he ordered 1,000,000 sesterces to be spent on his funeral.

Elder Pliny, *Natural History*, written mid first century AD

ℹ️ **Elder Pliny** Caius Pliny's uncle, Admiral Pliny, is known as the Elder Pliny, and Caius himself as the Younger Pliny. The Elder Pliny lived from about AD 23 to 79. He served in the army and as an administrator before he took command of the fleet at Misenum. In his spare time he wrote books. The only one to survive is his 37-volume Natural History which is an encyclopeadia of his knowledge – a lot of it wrong – of the earth and its peoples, plants and animals.

activity

1 Look at source 11.
a Was Caius Isidorus more or less rich than Caius Pliny?
b Was he a citizen, a freedman, or a slave?
2 With a partner work out whether each of the following statements are true or false:
● It was possible to be a Roman citizen and very rich.
● It was possible to be a Roman citizen and very poor.
● It was not possible to be very rich unless you were a Roman citizen.
● It was not possible to own slaves unless you were a Roman citizen.
Check your answers with other pairs.

Social classes

When historians study a society they sometimes describe it as being divided up into 'classes'. The word class comes from the Latin word 'classis' which meant 'rank' or 'order'. So each class is a group of people who all have the same position of importance, or rank.

The class of Roman society that you belonged to depended on two things:

1 Whether you were a freeborn Roman citizen or a slave.
2 The value of your property and your family background.

There were six classes of Roman society: the top four were for citizens, the bottom two were for slaves and freedmen. Source 12 shows how the system worked. The words in brackets are the Latin words for each class.

SOURCE 12

> Upper classes
>
> Freeborn Roman Citizens (cives Romani)
> 1. Senators (senatores) had to be worth at least 1,000,000 sesterces
> 2. Knights (equites) had to be worth at least 400,000 sesterces
>
> Lower classes
>
> 3. Ordinary citizens (Plebii)
> 4. Poorest citizens
>
> Slaves (servi)
> 5. Freedmen (libertis)
> 6. Slaves

A Senator was a member of the Senate, the council that advised the Emperor. There were only 600 senators. They were chosen from the sons of senators, from members of non-senatorial families, who had followed successful careers, and from people put forward by the Emperor. No one could become a senator unless he owned property worth at least 1 million sesterces (see source 12).

The next class, the Knights, was so called because originally this was the rank of citizens which had provided horsemen for the Roman army.

activity

3 Decide to which class of Roman society each of the following belonged:
● Caius Pliny (information on pages 39–40)
● The baker from Pompeii (see source 7 and information on page 38, and source 12 on page 23)
● Caius Isidorus (source 11)
4 To which class could Marcus Balbus (source 41 on page 34) have belonged? What do you need to know in order to be certain about his exact class?
5 Take the case of the baker (source 7).
a What clues are there in Parts 2 and 3 about how wealthy he might have been?
b He belonged to the fifth class of Roman society. Do you think he was better or worse off than freeborn citizens in the fourth and third classes?

The family

SOURCE 13

This carving from the side of a Roman tomb shows the upbringing of a Roman boy. It runs like a strip cartoon. The pictures show:
1 The boy being nursed by his mother.
2 The father takes the boy in his arms.
3 The boy learns to drive a goat-cart.
4 He goes to school.

Men ran Roman society. Even women who were freeborn Roman citizens could not vote, nor were they allowed to serve as town councillors. They were not allowed to be magistrates; nor to work in the government. They were not supposed to go out and earn their own living, but you have already seen some evidence that women from the lower classes could help to run a business.

Roman fathers were the head of the household and everyone had to do as they said. Until they were married girls had very little freedom. But they could marry from the age of 12 and many were married very young. Usually boys and girls had to marry whoever their father chose for them.

Once they were married, girls had much more freedom and people held them in respect. Wives organised the running of the household and shared their husband's authority. They could move freely around the city on their own or, if they were wealthy, escorted by slaves.

Roman women could own their own property and do what they liked with it rather than what their husbands told them to do. Married women in Britain first received that right only just over 100 years ago.

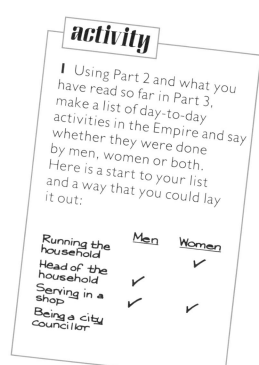

activity

1 Using Part 2 and what you have read so far in Part 3, make a list of day-to-day activities in the Empire and say whether they were done by men, women or both. Here is a start to your list and a way that you could lay it out:

	Men	Women
Running the household		✓
Head of the household	✓	
Serving in a shop	✓	✓
Being a city councillor	✓	

Religion

The family gods

SOURCE 14

The goddess Isis painted on the corridor leading to the lavatory in a shop in Pompeii.

On a wall outside the lavatory in a shop selling food and drink in Pompeii there was a painting of a goddess (source 14). The owner had it put there to make sure people's visits to the lavatory were pleasant and satisfactory.

The Romans believed in many gods and goddesses. They thought that each one was in charge of a different area of human life. If you wanted something to go well you had to have the right god or goddess on your side.

They thought every family was looked after by its own special gods. So every house had a place set aside in the corner of the hall (source 15) where the family kept statues of their gods.

The main ones were the Lares who looked after the house and the family; and the Penates who looked after the store cupboard and made sure that there was enough food. The head of the household went to this shrine every day to make offerings of food and wine on behalf of the family.

The Romans also believed that every family had a special power, or quality, called its 'genius', which was handed down from father to son. Noble families had **busts** made of ancestors who had served the family or the Empire especially well. They kept them in the

> **i** **Busts** A bust is a piece of sculpture representing the head, shoulders and chest of a person.

entrance hall and made offerings to them every day so that they would give their power to the present household. They also paraded them at funerals (source 16).

SOURCE 15

A shrine for family gods found in Herculaneum. The bottom part held the owner's ornaments. The top part was made to look like a temple. The tiny statues inside are the gods of the household.

SOURCE 16

The head of a noble household holding busts of two of his ancestors.

The gods of Rome

The Romans thought of their gods as super-humans who made friends and quarrelled just like humans, but never died. They borrowed this idea from the Greeks and they took over some of the Greek gods. In the end they came to see the chief Roman gods and goddesses as the same as the Greek ones who lived on Mount Olympus and controlled all that went on in the world. They aimed to please them so that Rome and the Empire would do well and prosper.

SOURCE 17

Jupiter, king of the gods (Greek name: Zeus). Also the god of the sky and the weather.

SOURCE 18

Mars, god of war (Greek name: Ares).

SOURCE 19

Neptune, god of the sea (Greek name: Poseidon). He also caused earthquakes by banging his trident.

SOURCE 20

Apollo, god of the sun. A Greek god whom the Romans worshipped directly. Also the god of prophecy – the art of telling what will happen in the future. Sometimes called Phoebus – 'shining one'.

SOURCE 21

Vulcan, god of metalworking (Greek name: Hephaistos). The Romans believed he made thunderbolts for Jupiter under Mount Etna in Sicily. Etna sometimes erupts like Vesuvius.

SOURCE 22

Mercury, god of communications (Greek name: Hermes). The messenger of the gods who looked after travellers, merchants and people engaged in trade and business. Businesspeople wanted him on their side so that they would earn large profits.

SOURCE 23

Juno, queen of the gods (Greek name: Hera). One special job was to look after women in childbirth.

SOURCE 24

Minerva, goddess of science and crafts (Greek name: Athene).

SOURCE 25

Diana, goddess of the moon and hunting (Greek name: Artemis).

SOURCE 26

Ceres, goddess of agriculture (Greek name: Demeter). Started as a goddess of corn and then became goddess of agriculture in general.

SOURCE 27

Venus, goddess of love (Greek name: Aphrodite).

SOURCE 28

Vesta, goddess of fire (Greek name: Hestia). Here she is shown blessing a marriage. There was a temple to Vesta in the centre of Rome with a sacred flame which stood for the life of the city.

activity

1 Look at sources 17 to 28.
a 'Cereal', 'volcano' and 'martial' are English words that come from the names of Roman gods or goddesses. Which name does each one come from?
b Why might a telephone company decide to call itself 'Mercury'?

Priests

The job of the priests was to make sure that the gods were on the side of the Romans. The Romans called this working to win 'the peace of the gods'.

They did this by making offerings of food, milk or wine. Sometimes they killed an animal and offered its body. This was called a 'sacrifice'. The priest had to make sure that exactly the right words and actions were carried out each time. If he made a mistake, it would block out the power of the god.

Being a priest did not mean that you had to lead a special way of life. The head of the household made the offerings at home. He was the priest for his own family and he passed on his knowledge to his son.

In the same way city councillors were chosen to act as priests for the people of their city. They made offerings and sacrifices in the open air, often on altars just outside the entrance to a temple.

The Romans thought of a temple as a house for god, like the shrines in their homes for the Lares and Penates. No one had to go there to worship. It was not like a church. The important thing was that the priest should make offerings at the right time and in the correct way.

SOURCE 29

Vestal Virgins on their way to sacrifice a pig at a festival. The Vestal Virgins were six girls from senators' families who had the job of looking after the sacred flame in the temple of Vesta. The Romans believed great harm would come to the city if it went out. Each priestess had to serve the goddess for thirty years and was not allowed to marry in that time. The punishment for breaking this rule was to be buried alive.

SOURCE 30

Inspecting the insides of a bull. The Romans tried to find out the will of the gods by studying 'omens' or signs. Special priests called 'augurs' looked for omens in the flight of birds and by examining the size, shape and colour of the organs inside an animal after it had been sacrificed.

assignments

I Using everything you have found out so far about the Roman people write as detailed an answer as you can to each of these questions:
a If you had been a man living in the Empire would you rather have been a poor citizen or a well-off freedman?
b If you had been a woman would you rather have been married to a poor citizen or a well-off freedman?
Explain your reasons as fully as possible in each case.

2a Which sources in Part 3 are from stones or monuments put up in memory of the dead?
b Make a list of the different sorts of information about the Roman people these sources provide.
c How useful do you think this kind of source is for finding out about the people of the Empire? Explain your reasons.

3a Look at source 6. Pliny's letter contains information about the attack on Masedo and also his opinions about this event.
 (i) Find an example of Pliny giving information.
 (ii) Find an example of Pliny giving his opinion.
(iii) Do you think that it is more important for us to know what happened or to have Pliny's opinions about these events?
b Look at source 5. Pliny's letter shows that he treated his slaves well.
 (i) Why might you need other evidence to be sure that Pliny did treat his slaves well?
(ii) What other evidence would help you to be sure?
c Pliny did not intend his letters to be used hundreds of years later by people trying to find out about slaves in his time. Does that mean his letters are not useful as evidence about slaves?

assignments

4 Images of Rome.

SOURCE 31

A painting called 'The Consummation of the Empire' by Thomas Cole who lived 1801–48.

SOURCE 32

A scene from the film *Spartacus*.

Sources 31 and 32 are examples of how a painter and a film-maker have shown their ideas of what Rome and its people were like in the days of the Empire. For each source:
a (i) Describe the impression given of Rome and its people.
(ii) Explain how this impression is built up.
b Use what you have found out in Parts 1, 2 and 3 to say what you think is (i) accurate, and (ii) inaccurate about this impression. Explain your reasons.

4

The Rise of the Roman Empire

Every Roman child had to know the story of how Rome came to rule an empire. We know from Pliny's letters that this was exactly what he was studying at his uncle's house the day Vesuvius erupted. He was reading a book by the historian **Livy** who wrote a history of Rome from the foundation of the city, in the seventh century BC, up to 9 BC.

Livy told how the earliest Romans were ruled by kings starting with Romulus (who was said to be the founder of the city), how the people eventually drove out the kings, and how Rome became a republic, which is a form of government in which the people choose the rulers. The Roman Republic lasted until 27 BC. After that, Rome had a single supreme ruler called an emperor.

SOURCE 1

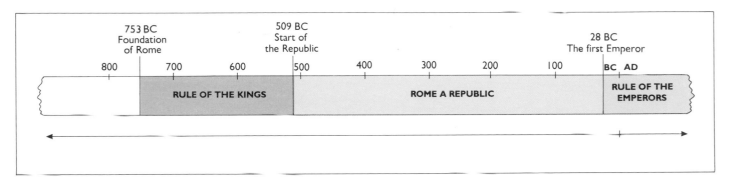

753 BC
Foundation of Rome

509 BC
Start of the Republic

28 BC
The first Emperor

800   700   600   500   400   300   200   100   BC AD

RULE OF THE KINGS   ROME A REPUBLIC   RULE OF THE EMPERORS

SOURCE 2

Roman legend told how twin baby boys, called Romulus and Remus, were abandoned on the banks of the River Tiber. A she-wolf found them and saved them by treating them as her cubs. They were rescued by shepherds who brought them up in the hills by the river where they later founded Rome. Afterwards Romulus killed Remus in a quarrel and ruled alone as the first king. This coin, made in 269 BC shows the she-wolf with the twins.

i **Livy** Titus Livius, known to English historians as Livy, lived from 59 BC to AD 17. His history of Rome, entitled Books from the Founding of Rome, filled 142 books but only 35 have survived. It was a favourite text book in Roman schools because as well as telling the story of Rome, Livy went out of his way to point out those qualities in the Roman people that had brought them their success.

The growth of Rome's Empire

Rome ruled an empire long before it had an emperor. Source 3 shows you how the size of the lands Rome ruled grew in the time of the Republic.

SOURCE 3a

The Empire in 264 BC. In the early days of the Republic the Romans were mainly peaceful farmers; but the tribes living in the nearby hills wanted their rich lands. So the Romans had to fight to defend them. They became good fighters and went on the attack to drive their enemies away. They defeated them one by one. Instead of taking over their enemies' lands they allowed them to keep them and in return asked them to become friends and allies. By about 300 BC the various tribes of Italy were living together, fairly peacefully, under Roman leadership.

SOURCE 3b

The Empire in 201 BC. In 264 BC Rome went to war with Carthage, a rival city in North Africa. The Carthaginians were a rich sea-faring people who traded all over the Mediterranean. They had also settled in lands on the coasts of North Africa, Southern Spain and France. The war lasted on-and-off for 65 years. The Romans suffered many defeats; but in the end they won and took over all the Carthaginian territory.

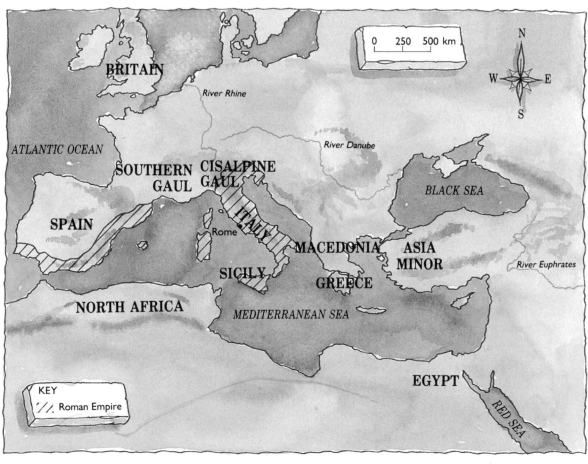

SOURCE 3c

The Empire in 121 BC. After the war against Carthage, Roman armies started to fight in the lands around the eastern Mediterranean. By 121 BC they had conquered Macedonia, Greece and Asia Minor, and had arranged a treaty of friendship with Egypt. Many other rulers of lands along the Mediterranean coasts had become Rome's allies.

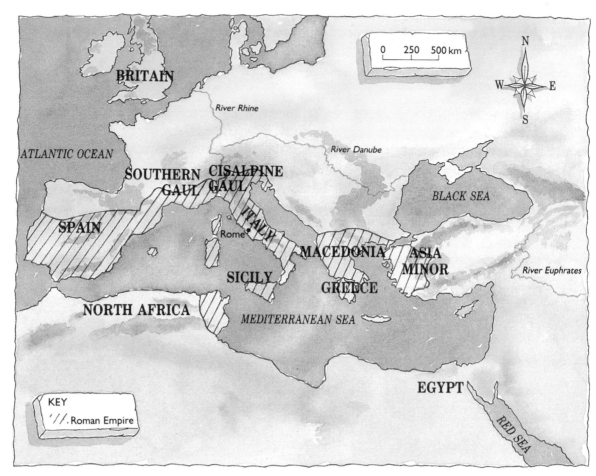

SOURCE 3d

The Empire in AD 14. By AD 14 the Romans had conquered new territories to both the east and the west. They now controlled almost the whole of the coastline of the Mediterranean as well as the lands in Gaul (modern France) and Germany.

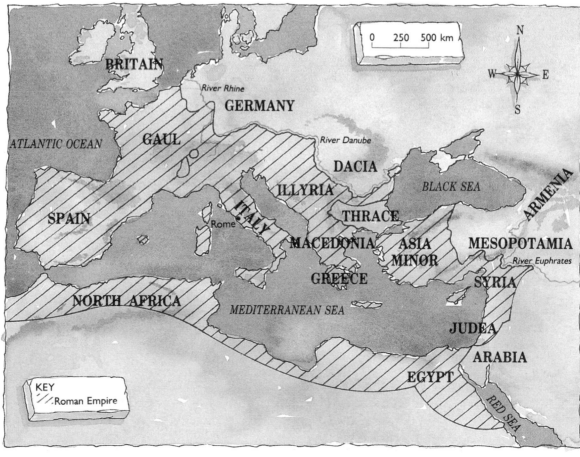

Why did the Romans gain an empire?

You can see from the information in source 3 that the Romans used two main methods to build their empire:

1 They defeated other peoples and took over their lands.
2 They made alliances with the rulers of other countries who agreed to obey them.

That tells you <u>how</u> the Romans built their empire; but it doesn't tell you <u>why</u> they wanted an empire in the first place, or why they were successful in building one.

When you ask a question such as 'Why did the Romans want an empire?' or 'Why were they successful in building one up?', you are trying to find out reasons for something happening in the past.

A reason why something happens is called a 'cause'. The event it helps to make happen is called a 'result' or 'consequence'. In the rest of Part 4 you are going to look at some possible causes of the fact that the Romans came to rule an empire.

Camillus and the Faliscans

In the early days of the Republic, the Romans fought against neighbouring tribes in Italy. An army led by Camillus went to fight a people called the Faliscans. They quickly retreated into their city. Camillus surrounded it and started a siege.

The leaders of the Faliscans employed a teacher for their sons. He used to take them to play outside the city gates. Sometimes he kept them close to the gates, sometimes he took them further away. One day he kept the boys playing and talking until they reached the outposts of the Roman army.

SOURCE 4

Then he took them to Camillus in the headquarter's tent . . . He told Camillus that he was handing over the boys . . . so as to give the Romans power over the city.

. . . Camillus replied, 'You are a villain. I and the Roman people are not like you. We have learnt to fight our wars in a just way. You are trying to overcome the chief men of your city by an act of treachery; but I shall conquer them by Roman arts, by courage and strategy [clever plans] and force of arms.'

Livy, *Books from the Founding of Rome*, written between about 89 BC and AD 17

Camillus ordered his soldiers to strip the teacher of his clothes and tie his hands behind his back. Then he handed him back to the boys, gave them sticks, and told them to whip the traitor back into the city:

SOURCE 5

The people came in crowds to watch . . . Everyone was talking about the Roman sense of honour and their commander's love of justice.

Then the chief men of the Faliscans went to the Senate in Rome and said, 'Senators. We surrender ourselves to you, for we think it better to live under your rule than under our own laws . . . '

Livy, *Books from the Founding of Rome*, written between about 89 BC and AD 17

activity

2 Look at sources 4 and 5 and the information with them.

a What did Camillus do when the teacher brought the boys to him?

b Why do you think he reacted like this?

c What reasons did the chief men of Faliscans give for surrendering to the Senate in Rome?

d What clues does this story give you about why Italian tribes were often prepared to accept Roman rule?

i　Quinqueremes and triremes　Warships invented by the Greeks. They were powered by oars and sails. A quinquereme had five banks of oars, one above the other, and a trireme had three. Both had decks above the rowers for soldiers, and a sharp metal ram at the front for sinking enemy ships.

i　Polybius　Polybius was a Greek historian born in about 200 BC. He became friends with the Scipio family in Rome and was with Scipio Aemilianus when he captured and destroyed Carthage in 146 BC. He wrote The Rise of the Roman Empire to try to explain how 'the Romans succeeded in less than fifty-three years (220 BC–167 BC) in bringing under their rule almost the whole of the inhabited world, an achievement which is without parallel in human history.'

The Romans build a navy

During their first war with Carthage, between 264 and 241 BC, the Romans realised that the Carthaginians had a big advantage because they had a fleet that controlled the Mediterranean Sea.

Even though the Romans were not a seafaring people, they decided to build warships – one hundred **quinqueremes** and twenty **triremes**. The problem was that quinquiremes had never been used in Italy before, so their ship builders had no idea of how to build one:

SOURCE 6

The Romans had no resources for the job. Up to now they had never given a thought to the sea. But once they had the idea they went ahead so boldly that they immediately took on the Carthaginians.

Earlier on, one of the Carthaginians' quinqueremes had run aground. The Romans had captured it and now they used it as a model . . . Those who had been given the task of shipbuilding busied themselves with the construction work, while others collected the crews and began to train them to row on shore.

They placed the men along the rowers' benches on dry land, seating them in the same order as if they were in an actual vessel. Then they stationed the under-officers in the middle and trained the oarsmen to row as a team . . .

Polybius, *The Rise of the Roman Empire*, written towards the end of the second century BC

activity

1a　Why does Polybius (source 6) think that the Romans' decision to build a fleet was a very bold one?
b　The Romans' success in building a fleet of ships and training sailors was partly the result of good luck and partly of good organisation. Make one list of things that showed their good luck and another of things that showed their good organisation. Which do you think was the most important?

The Romans invent a weapon

Carthaginian ships were faster and easier to move about than Roman ships, and they had strong battering rams at the front which they used to sink the enemy. The Romans found it very difficult to win a sea battle so they invented a device called the 'raven' to try to gain an advantage.

SOURCE 7

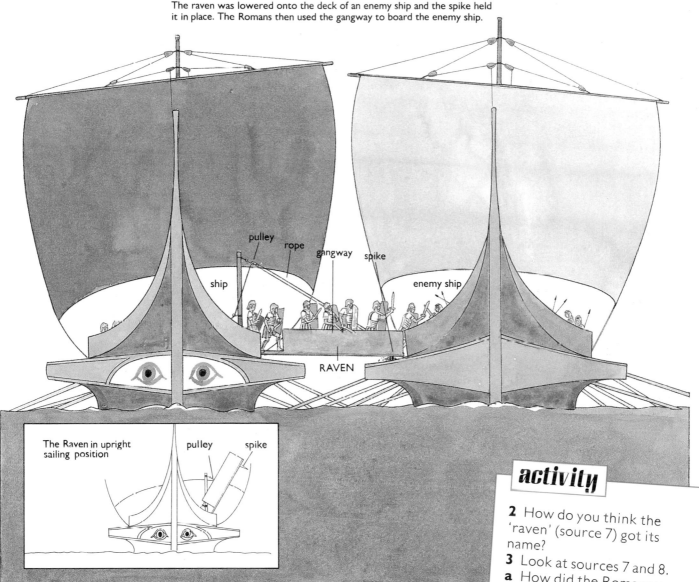

The raven was lowered onto the deck of an enemy ship and the spike held it in place. The Romans then used the gangway to board the enemy ship.

pulley   rope   gangway   spike

ship   enemy ship

RAVEN

The Raven in upright sailing position   pulley   spike

The 'raven'. An artist's reconstruction based on a description by the historian Polybuis.

Polybius described the sea battle when the Romans first used the 'raven':

SOURCE 8

When the Carthaginians first saw the 'ravens' hoisted aloft in the Roman ships, they did not know what to make of them . . . As they despised the Romans they attacked without hesitation. Then . . . they found their ships held by the 'ravens' and Roman troops swarmed aboard over the gangways and fought them hand-to-hand on deck.

The result was that the Carthaginians lost every one of the first thirty of their ships that went into the battle, crews and all.

Polybius, *The Rise of the Roman Empire,* written towards the end of the second century BC

activity

2 How do you think the 'raven' (source 7) got its name?

3 Look at sources 7 and 8.

a How did the Romans use the 'raven'?

b How did the 'raven' help the Romans?

c The Romans knew that the Carthaginians had better ships and more experienced sailors. What does the story of the 'raven' tell you about the way the Romans thought about how to win battles?

4 The Romans had never had a navy before. What do sources 6, 7, and 8 tell you about the way the Romans faced completely new problems?

activity

1 Look at sources 9, 10 and 11. Make a list of the qualities the Romans most looked for in their soldiers.
2 Look at sources 10 and 11. Do you think that these ways of **a** rewarding and **b** punishing soldiers worked?
3 What evidence is there in Source 10 that all Romans placed a very high value on being a good soldier?

The Roman army

Polybius thought that another reason why the Romans gained an empire was the strength and discipline of their army.

The Roman army was organised into four large regiments, called legions, of between 4,000 and 5,000 men. Each legion was divided into thirty companies commanded by two officers called centurions.

SOURCE 9

In choosing their centurions the Romans look not so much for the daring type but rather for men who are natural leaders, who will stand their ground when hard pressed and will die in defence of their posts.

Polybius, *The Rise of the Roman Empire*, written towards the end of the second century BC

Polybius was impressed by the way in which the Romans rewarded courage and punished cowardice:

SOURCE 10

The Romans have an excellent method of encouraging young soldiers to face danger. The general assembles the troops and calls forward those he considers to have shown exceptional bravery.

He praises them . . . and then he gives out gifts . . . At the storming of a city the first man to scale [climb] the wall is awarded a crown of gold.

The men who receive these trophies enjoy great prestige [honour and glory] in the army and afterwards in their own homes. They are also chosen to take the lead in religious processions when they return home.

Polybius, *The Rise of the Roman Empire*, written towards the end of the second century BC

SOURCE 11

If it ever happens that a whole company of men desert their posts under great pressure in battle, the tribune [a senior officer] calls the legion on parade and brings to the front those who are guilty of having left the ranks.

*He then chooses, by **drawing lots**, about one in ten of all those who have shown themselves guilty of cowardice. They are then clubbed to death.*

Polybius, *The Rise of the Roman Empire*, written towards the end of the second century BC

i **Drawing lots** An ancient method of making a decision by chance. The tribune put one wooden stick for each soldier who had been cowardly into a bag. One stick out of every ten was shorter than the rest. The sticks were shaken and the soldiers had to draw one each from the bag. The soldiers who drew the short sticks were the ones who had to die.

The rewards of conquest

The Romans had a law saying that when an army conquered a new territory all the booty had to go to the general. He was supposed to give some to the Treasury in Rome, some to his own soldiers and to use some to put up buildings in Rome for everyone to use. One writer reported that after the conquest of Macedonia, one Roman took home 250 waggons full of statues and paintings.

The Romans divided the lands that they conquered into provinces. A governor, who was sent from Rome, ruled each province. He appointed tax collectors to collect the taxes due to Rome. Some governors made a lot of money for themselves by arranging for the collectors to demand extra money which he would split with them.

SOURCE 12

This Roman mosaic shows slaves working on a large country estate. The Romans took thousands of prisoners of war back to Italy and sold them as slaves. These prisoners were part of the general's booty. The island of Delos in the Aegean Sea became a trading centre for slaves. In around 100 BC Delos was handling 10,000 slaves a day.

SOURCE 13

activity

1 Look at the information on page 59 and sources 12 and 13.
a Make a list of all the rewards the Romans got from conquest.
b Do you think that these rewards went to all Romans or just some Romans. Who do you think benefited the most?
2 What does source 13 tell you about how Romans gained by ruling southern Gaul? Which Romans benefited most in this case do you think?

The wreck of a Roman ship that sank off the south coast of France in the first century BC on its way to Gaul from Italy with a cargo of pottery and wine. This photograph was taken when the archaeologists were in the middle of removing the cargo. You can see the clay jars that held the wine. Archaeologists have also found the wrecks of ships on their way to Rome from the eastern Mediterranean. These contained works of art such as statues.

assignments

1a Work in pairs
(i) divide up these headings from Part 4 so that each pair has <u>two</u> and each heading is given to at least one pair:

Camillus and the Faliscans
The Romans build a navy
The Romans invent a weapon
The Roman army
The rewards of conquest

(ii) Decide how the sources and information under your two headings help to explain why the Romans gained an empire.
(iii) Make a list of your ideas.
b Discuss your ideas with other pairs.
c Work as a class to make a list of all the causes that you think led to Rome gaining an empire.
d (i) Work in pairs again to decide which you think were the most important causes and which the least important.
(ii) Discuss your decisions with the rest of the class. Does everyone agree?

From Republic to Empire

The word 'empire' has two meanings. The first is 'a very large area of land ruled by one country'. So, when we talk about the Roman Empire, we mean all the territory ruled over by Rome.

The second meaning is 'a territory ruled over by someone called an emperor'. An emperor is someone who rules alone and has a lot of power, like a king.

The interesting thing about the Roman Empire is that it started out as an empire in the first sense of the word, and then became an empire in the second sense too.

Until 27 BC Rome was a republic which means that the people chose their rulers. From 27 BC onwards, Rome was ruled by an emperor.

Rome as a republic

In the Roman Republic the citizens met once a year to elect the city's officials. Chief of these were two 'consuls' whose job was to run the affairs of the city for the year. They also acted as generals.

The consuls took advice from a council of experienced men called the **Senate**, and they then went on to become lifetime members of the Senate once their period of office was over. The Senate could only advise but it had a lot of power because consuls ruled for only one year and often relied on the experience of the Senators.

An important rule was that either consul had the power to stop the other from taking an action with which he disagreed. He could say, no. The Latin for 'I say no' is 'veto'. We still use veto as an English word today.

The citizens also elected magistrates called 'tribunes' to serve for one year. Their job was to protect ordinary people against unfair laws or actions. They did not have the power to make laws, but they could veto the actions of any citizen or magistrate including the consuls.

> **i** **Senate** The word 'senate' comes from the Latin word 'senex' meaning an old man'.

The rise of the generals

In 100 BC a consul called Marius completely reorganised the army. Till then it had consisted of citizens who joined up when the consuls needed them for a war and went home once the war was over. Marius created a professional army. Soldiers were paid and had to join up for at least sixteen years.

Marius also made his soldiers swear an oath of loyalty, not to Rome as was usual, but to him personally. Other generals did the same. Now it was possible for a general and his army to become strong enough to disobey the Senate. They might even decide to take Rome over and rule by force.

Some people feared the increase in the power of the generals. They were right to do this: two generals, Pompey and Julius Caesar, both conquered new lands without the direct orders of the Senate. It made them popular with their soldiers who wanted booty and with the ordinary people who were excited by the triumphal processions and displays when the armies returned home.

SOURCE 1

Pompey.

SOURCE 2

Julius Caesar.

Julius Caesar becomes dictator

In 49 BC Julius Caesar returned from Gaul at the head of his army. The people of Rome cheered him through the streets, but Pompey and many senators feared that he would take over as ruler of Rome.

Pompey formed an army to oppose Caesar; but Caesar defeated it and in 45 BC made himself the sole ruler of Rome. He took the title 'dictator' which means someone whose rule is law. Some senators thought he meant to make himself king and to hand on his power to his family. That would mean the end of the Republic for ever.

Even the common people started to fear Caesar's rule. They openly asked for someone to come forward and stand up for their ancient freedoms, especially the the right to choose their leaders.

The murder of Caesar

A group of Senators, led by Gaius Cassius and Marcus Brutus, banded together and planned to attack Caesar at a meeting of the Senate. As soon as Caesar took his place on his seat of state the small band of plotters crowded round as if to pay their respects. One came up close, pretending to ask a question. Caesar waved him away but he caught hold of Caesar's shoulders:

SOURCE 3

> 'This is violence,' Caesar cried, and at that moment one of the Casca brothers slipped behind . . . and stabbed him just below the throat.
>
> Caesar grasped Casca's arm and ran it through with his own knife; he was leaping away when another dagger caught him in the chest. Confronted by a ring of drawn daggers, he drew the top of his gown over his face . . . Twenty-three dagger thrusts went home [into him] as he stood there . . .
>
> The entire Senate then went away in confusion and Caesar was left lying dead . . . until three of his household slaves carried him home . . .
>
> Suetonius, *The Twelve Caesars*, written early second century AD

Brutus and Cassius hoped to save the Republic by killing Caesar. They failed because Mark Anthony and Octavian, Caesar's great-nephew and adopted son, won the support of the people, took command of an army and defeated them.

They divided the Empire between them. Octavian ruled in the west and Anthony in the east, until they too quarrelled. Octavian defeated Anthony in a sea battle and Anthony committed suicide.

The first emperor

When Octavian returned to Rome he gave himself the title 'Emperor', and he added the title 'Augustus', which means 'his majesty', to his family name, Caesar. Augustus Caesar ruled as Rome's first emperor from 28 BC to AD 14.

Augustus needed to have the power of a king, but he also wanted the Roman people to feel that the new office of emperor fitted in with the way things were done in the old days, before the civil wars between the generals, when the Republic had been strong.

You can see from source 4 how he managed to do that. The Senate carried on and the people once again elected magistrates. But the Emperor was now at the centre of government and controlled everything. He held the most important jobs such as commander-in-chief of the army and chief priest. He was elected consul for life. Yet he did not put himself obviously above everyone else the way Julius Caesar had done. Instead of using the title 'Emperor', Augustus called himself 'Princeps', which means, 'First Citizen'.

SOURCE 4

THE REPUBLIC

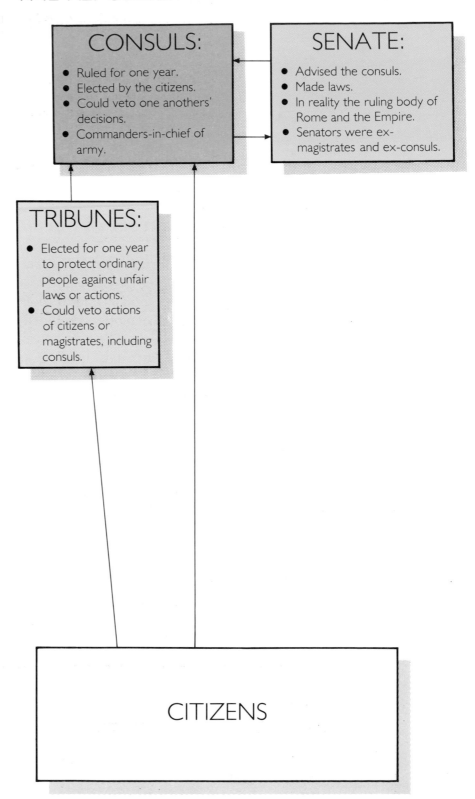

CONSULS:
- Ruled for one year.
- Elected by the citizens.
- Could veto one anothers' decisions.
- Commanders-in-chief of army.

SENATE:
- Advised the consuls.
- Made laws.
- In reality the ruling body of Rome and the Empire.
- Senators were ex-magistrates and ex-consuls.

TRIBUNES:
- Elected for one year to protect ordinary people against unfair laws or actions.
- Could veto actions of citizens or magistrates, including consuls.

CITIZENS

The change from the Republic to the Empire.

THE EMPIRE

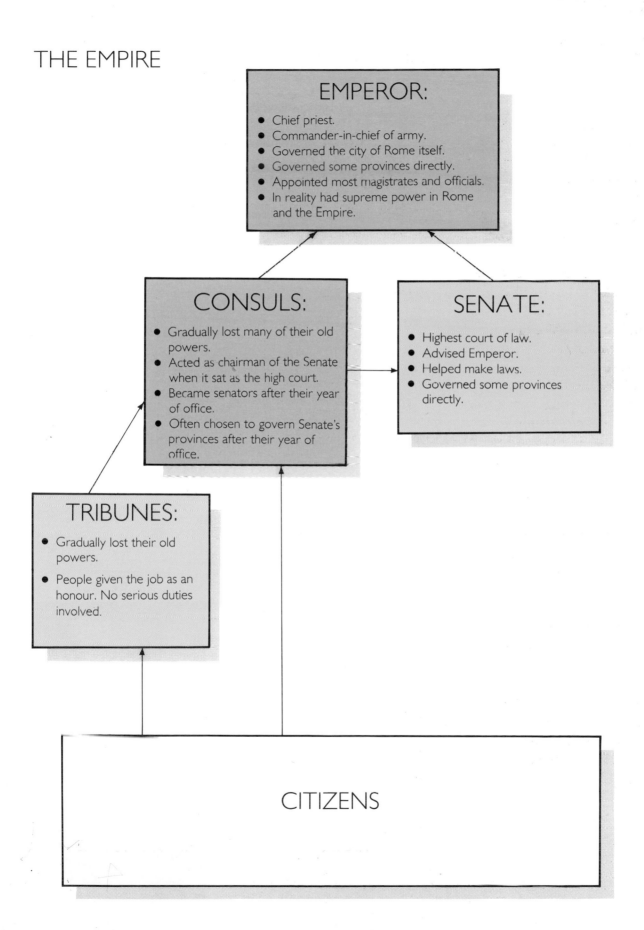

EMPEROR:
- Chief priest.
- Commander-in-chief of army.
- Governed the city of Rome itself.
- Governed some provinces directly.
- Appointed most magistrates and officials.
- In reality had supreme power in Rome and the Empire.

CONSULS:
- Gradually lost many of their old powers.
- Acted as chairman of the Senate when it sat as the high court.
- Became senators after their year of office.
- Often chosen to govern Senate's provinces after their year of office.

SENATE:
- Highest court of law.
- Advised Emperor.
- Helped make laws.
- Governed some provinces directly.

TRIBUNES:
- Gradually lost their old powers.
- People given the job as an honour. No serious duties involved.

CITIZENS

SOURCE 5

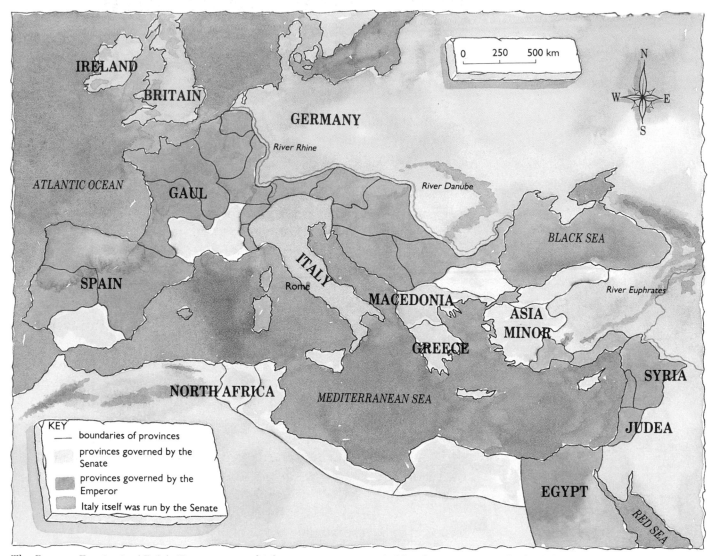

The Roman Empire in AD 14. You can see which provinces were ruled by the Emperor and which by the senate.

Augustus also arranged for the Emperor to share the government of the provinces of the Empire with the Senate and consuls (source 5).

activity

I Use the information on pages 61–65, and sources 4 and 6 to make lists of **a** the similarities, and **b** the differences between:
 (i) the Republic and the Empire;
(ii) Julius Caesar and Augustus Caesar.

SOURCE 6

Augustus Caesar. Why do you think he is shown wearing a toga? What message do you think this statue was meant to give the Roman people about Augustus as Emperor?

What kept the Empire together?

For 200 years from the time of Augustus, the Romans were so successful that they boasted you could travel from one end of the Empire to the other in complete safety. They believed the Empire stood for good order and peace, and people talked about 'Pax Romana', the peace of Rome.

Romans like Caius Pliny, living towards the end of the first century AD, took it for granted that Rome ruled lands outside Italy, and that it had done so for hundreds of years. But, if you think about it, it is not at all obvious that the Romans should have managed to hold on to all the territories they conquered and to govern them successfully.

How did they manage to do it? You can work out the answer in the rest of Part 5. Start by thinking about this idea:

Pliny probably thought of the Empire as something that was bound to hold together; but you could look at it another way and think of the Empire as something that was trying to fall apart.

Have you ever tried to put up a tent? If you have, I think you will agree that it is easy to think of a tent as something that is trying to fall down. You could quite easily make a list of things about a tent which make it want to fall down and another list of things which help it to stand up.

So before you go any further, work out the things that were trying to make the Roman Empire fall apart.

---

activity

2 Use source 2 in Part I and everything you have found out so far about the Roman Empire to make a list of all the things you can think of which were trying to make it fall apart. Here are some points to start your list:

- the Romans were outnumbered by the people whose lands they governed
- the people of the Empire spoke many different languages

3 Discuss your list with other people.

activity

la What do sources 7, 8 and 9 tell you about the job of being Emperor?

b What do sources 8 and 9 tell you about the way in which ordinary people in the provinces thought about the Emperor?

2 Make a list of all the ways in which you think the Emperor helped to hold the Empire together.

The Emperor

The first four emperors were related to Augustus. After that emperors were usually successful generals, though members of a family often succeeded one another. By the second century men from the provinces were accepted as emperors. Trajan and Hadrian, for example, both came from Spain.

Augustus had a long list of everything he had done inscribed on the sides of monuments:

SOURCE 7

I built . . . The Temple of Apollo . . . and the imperial box on the Circus Maximus . . . I repaired water channels which had become derelict with age in many places . . . and the Via Flaminia [a road] . . . I built the Temple of Mars . . . and the Forum of Augustus on land which I owned myself . . . From the spoils of war I consecrated [gave] gifts . . . the cost to myself was some 100,000,000 sesterces.

Augustus, *Res Gestae*, published after his death in AD 14

The Emperor was the centre of government. People came to see him to ask for favours:

SOURCE 8

My ship anchored at a Greek island and I noticed a little village where some fisherman lived. When we sailed one of them came on board. The village had elected him to go as their representative to Augustus Caesar, to try to get him to agree to reduce the tax that they had to pay.

Strabo, *Geography*, completed early first century AD

The Emperor Hadrian made a point of travelling all over the Empire to see what was going on for himself:

SOURCE 9

A woman put a request to Hadrian as he went past on one of his journeys. He answered, 'I've no time'. But when she shouted after him that in that case he had better stop being Emperor, he gave her the chance to put her case.

Cassius Dio, *Roman History*, completed early third century AD

Julius Caesar was worshipped as a god after his death and from Augustus's time emperors were usually made into gods when they died. Augustus also allowed his family spirit, or genius, to be worshipped while he was alive. People took oaths in his name and set up temples to 'Rome and Augustus'. In some eastern provinces he was even worshipped as a god while he was alive.

SOURCE 10

Immediately after the invasion of Britain in AD 43, work started on a temple to Emperor Claudius in Colchester. This model shows what it probably looked like. The Romans said that as long as you sacrificed to the gods of Rome including the Emperor and so showed your loyalty to the state, you could worship any other god you happened to choose as well.

The frontiers

Although Augustus advised his successors not to make the Empire any bigger, some of them decided to extend it. Claudius and Trajan both made further conquests. By the time of Trajan's death in 117, the Empire was at its largest.

His successor, Hadrian, spent more than thirteen years of his twenty-one-year rule outside Rome. He travelled round the Empire to see problems for himself. Hadrian concentrated on building up strong frontiers.

Hadrian decided to abandon those of Trajan's conquests which he thought would be too difficult and too expensive to defend. The rest he kept.

Often a river or the sea forms a frontier. These together with, for example, mountains are called natural frontiers. They are not made by people and they are easily defended. Where there was no natural frontier or it was not strong enough, the Romans built fortifications.

The Romans called those who lived outside the Empire 'barbarians'. They allowed them to cross the frontier to buy and sell goods in the markets as long as they were unarmed and under the supervision of the army.

They built army camps all along their frontiers. These became the centre of civilian settlements with their own shops, taverns and baths. Often soldiers married local girls and lived with them outside the camp. When they retired they might be given farms in the area.

> **Barbarians** This comes from the Latin word 'barbarus' which meant strange, foreign or uncivilised. The Romans borrowed it from the Greeks who thought people speaking other languages sounded as if they were stammering and saying 'bar-bar-bar'. So they used 'barbaros' – the Greek word for stammering – to mean foreign as well.

SOURCE 11

The Empire under Hadrian.

KEY
•••• man-made frontiers
▨ area conquered by Trajan, but abandoned by Hadrian

BRITAIN

River Rhine
German tribes

River Danube

ATLANTIC OCEAN

GAUL

DACIA

BLACK SEA

ARMENIA

SPAIN

Rome • ITALY

MACEDONIA

Byzantium

ASIA MINOR

River Euphrates

River Tigris

MESOPOTAMIA

GREECE

• Athens

• Antioch

NUMIDIA

AFRICA   MEDITERRANEAN SEA

SYRIA

SAHARA DESERT

Jerusalem •

Alexandria •   ARABIA

ARABIAN DESERT

EGYPT   RED SEA

0   250   500 km

activity

I Look at source 11.
a Which lands conquered by Trajan did Hadrian keep and which did he abandon? Explain why you think he did this.
b Make a list of all the natural frontiers of the Roman Empire at the time of Hadrian.
c Find the special fortifications built along the frontiers and say why you think the Romans built them in those particular places.
2 Look at source 12.
a What does it tell you about the importance of frontiers to the Romans?
b What do you think a frontier like this meant to the tribes living outside the Empire on the other side?
3 Make a list of ways in which the frontiers helped to hold the Empire together.

SOURCE 12

Hadrian's Wall in northern Britain. Hadrian ordered it to be built in AD 122 between the River Tyne and the Solway Firth. It is 73 miles (117 km) long, 4 metres high and wide enough to walk on. Sixteen forts were built into the wall every five miles (8 km) with eighty smaller mile castles filling in between them. A deep ditch guarded the front of the wall. A second ditch called a 'vallum' lay some distance behind it. The area between the wall and the vallum was a military zone. Travellers had to enter and leave it at controlled crossing places.

activity

4a What does source 13 tell you about the kind of training that Roman troops had to do?

b What most satisfied Hadrian about their performance?

c What does this tell you about the Roman army?

The army

The Roman army was admired for the quality of its equipment (source 14) and the training and discipline of the soldiers. In 128 the Emperor Hadrian went to review the training exercises of his troops in Africa. Afterwards he addressed them:

SOURCE 13

You did everything in due order; you covered the whole ground in your manoeuvres; your spear throwing was neat, though you used the short weapon which is difficult. Most of you were as good with the longer spear. Your jumping was lively today and yesterday it was swift. If you had fallen short in anything, I would call your attention to it; if you had shone in anything, I would remark on it, but in fact it was the even level of your performance which pleased me.

Part of Hadrian's speech to his troops, North Africa, 128

The army's main jobs were to make sure all the people of the provinces obeyed Roman orders, to guard the frontiers, to build and maintain the roads and forts needed for communication and defence, and, occasionally, to take over new territories beyond the frontiers.

SOURCE 14

Roman soldiers crossing a pontoon bridge over the River Danube into Dacia. Find:
- The standard bearers. Each legion had several standards including its own gold or silver eagle – the symbol of Jupiter, king of the gods. It was a great honour to carry it, and a great disgrace if the enemy captured it.
- The soldiers' equipment carried on poles over their shoulders. As well as his weapons every legionary had to carry three days' rations, cooking pots, an axe, a hammer, a spade, a basket for moving earth, a bag of nails, rope, and a cloak which doubled as a blanket.

Sometimes it had to deal with rebellions, as in AD 66 when the Jews rose up against Roman rule. By AD 73 the rebels were trapped in the mountain fortress of Masada (source 15), their last stronghold.

In order to take the fortress, the Romans built a wall 3,500 metres long around the base of the mountain and eight siege camps for the troops. Then they built a massive ramp of earth, paved it with stones and pushed a siege tower and a battering ram to the top.

On the night before the Roman's final attack all 960 defenders, except two women and five children, committed suicide.

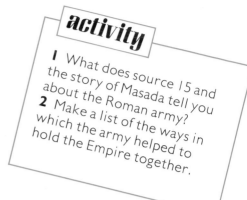

activity

1 What does source 15 and the story of Masada tell you about the Roman army?
2 Make a list of the ways in which the army helped to hold the Empire together.

SOURCE 15

The mountain-top fortress of Masada in modern Israel. Find:
● the remains of one of the Roman camps in the bottom of the picture
● the earth ramp in the centre

Roads

SOURCE 16

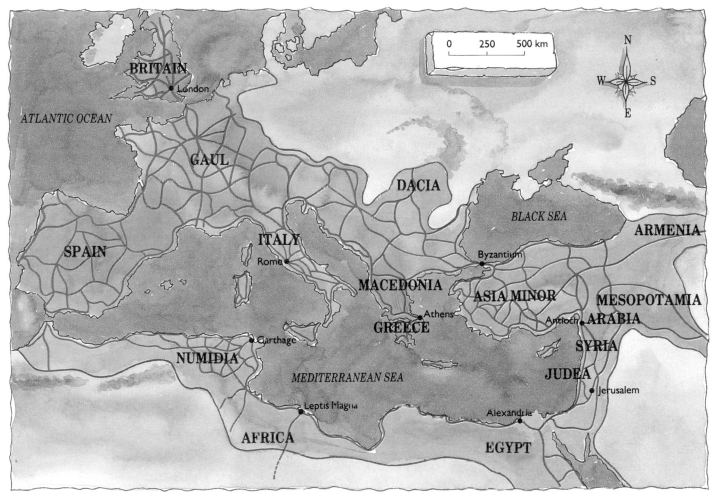

The roads of the Roman Empire in about AD 100.

In 312 BC a Roman official called Appius Claudius ordered a road to be built to connect Rome to Capua in the south so that the Romans could move troops and equipment quickly to any troublespot. It was named after him – the Via Appia – and it is the first Roman road of which we have a record.

Over the next 200 years, the Romans built roads all over Italy. By the end of the first century AD a network of roads connected every part of the Empire (source 16).

SOURCE 17

The Via Appia. It is still used today. On this section you can still see the original paving stones.

This road network totalled some 49,000 miles. Compare that to the United States of America today where the main motorways, known as the Interstate Highway system, total about 42,500 miles. It cost the Romans 500,000 sesterces to build one mile of road. That makes over 6 billion sesterces to pay for the whole lot. On top of that the surfaces had to be repaired every 30 to 40 years.

To begin with the roads were meant for the army. They soon became just as important for officials travelling on government business and Augustus set up a special government postal service called the Imperial Post:

SOURCE 18

So that reports of what was happening in all the provinces could be carried faster, the Emperor Augustus placed young men, first of all, and later coaches, at short intervals along the military roads. The idea of coaches was better because the same man could bring a message and be questioned about it.

Suetonius, *The Twelve Caesars*, written early second century AD

SOURCE 19

A coach of the Imperial Post. Find the official emblem on the side.

activity

1 Make a list of the different ways that roads helped to hold the Empire together.

Trade

The provinces of the Empire supplied Rome with everything from food, to slaves, to marble for buildings. As time passed, Rome grew more and more dependent on the provinces, especially for corn to make bread which came first from Egypt and then increasingly from North Africa.

The provinces could trade with each other as well as with Rome. Goods travelled all over the Empire by road and ship. Archaeologists have found that farmers living on the west coast of Wales used the same type of pottery as people living in the desert towns of Mesopotamia.

SOURCE 20

A boat taking corn from the port at Ostia up the River Tiber to Rome. The grain supply was of great importance to the people of Rome. Many of them were poor or unemployed and were given free bread. There were often riots if they did not get it. From a tomb painting in Ostia.

SOURCE 21

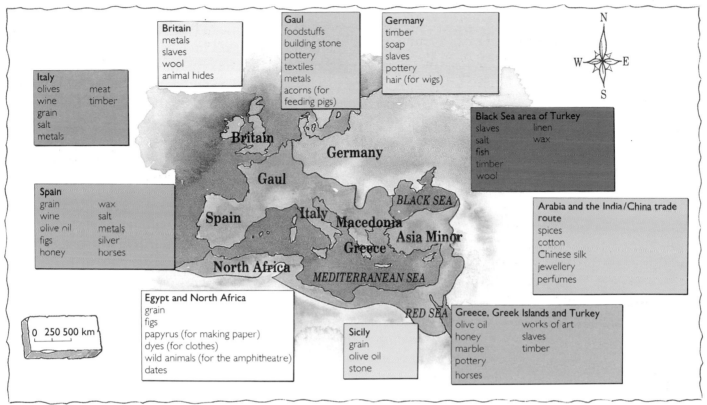

Italy
olives   meat
wine   timber
grain
salt
metals

Britain
metals
slaves
wool
animal hides

Gaul
foodstuffs
building stone
pottery
textiles
metals
acorns (for
feeding pigs)

Germany
timber
soap
slaves
pottery
hair (for wigs)

Black Sea area of Turkey
slaves   linen
salt   wax
fish
timber
wool

Spain
grain   wax
wine   salt
olive oil   metals
figs   silver
honey   horses

**Arabia and the India/China trade
route**
spices
cotton
Chinese silk
jewellery
perfumes

Egypt and North Africa
grain
figs
papyrus (for making paper)
dyes (for clothes)
wild animals (for the amphitheatre)
dates

Sicily
grain
olive oil
stone

Greece, Greek Islands and Turkey
olive oil   works of art
honey   slaves
marble   timber
pottery
horses

0 250 500 km

The goods supplied by the provinces of the Empire in the first century AD.

SOURCE 22

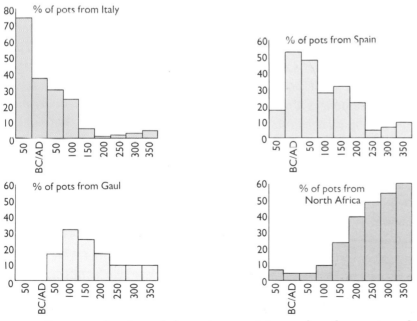

In Roman times merchants used clay pots as containers when they sent goods by ship. Archaeologists discovered hundreds of these pots buried at Ostia which was Rome's seaport. They worked out where each pot came from by looking at the markings on its side. These graphs show what percentage of the pots came from particular parts of the Empire at different times. You can use them to work out which parts of the Empire were sending out the most pots, and so doing the most trade with Rome at different times.

activity

2 Look at source 22.
a Was Italy selling more things or fewer things to the Empire in AD 100 than in 100 BC?
b Which provinces sent most to Rome in (i) AD 100, (ii) AD 200, and (iii) AD 300?
c How are these graphs evidence that (i) Rome depended on the provinces for food supplies, and (ii) Rome depended on different provinces at different times.
3 Use the information and sources 20–22 to make a list of the ways in which trade helped to hold the Empire together.

Pliny governs his province

In 111 the Emperor Trajan sent Caius Pliny to Bithynia and Pontus as his special representative. This province, which lay along the south coast of the Black Sea, was causing the Emperor problems. Pliny's job was to sort things out. The letters that Pliny and Trajan sent one another are full of clues to the way the Romans governed the Empire:

SOURCE 23

a) Pliny to Trajan:

I pray you, Sir, to advise me . . . whether to continue the custom of using the public slaves in the various towns as prison warders, or to put soldiers on guard-duty in the prisons.

b) Trajan to Pliny:

There is no need, my dear Pliny, for more soldiers to be transferred to guard-duty in the prisons. We should continue the custom of the province and use public slaves as warders . . . Let us . . . keep to the general rule that as few soldiers as possible should be called away from active service.

SOURCE 24

a) Pliny to Trajan:

In several cities there are people who were sentenced to service in the mines . . . but who are now performing the duties of public slaves and receiving an annual salary for their work . . . I have been wondering what to do. I felt it was too hard on the men to send them back to work out their sentences after so many years, when most of them are old by now, and by all accounts are quietly leading honest lives, but I did not think it quite right to retain criminals in public service.

b) Trajan to Pliny:

Let us not forget the chief reason for sending you to your province was the need for many reforms. Nothing . . . stands more in need of correction than the situation described in your letter . . . Those among them who were sentenced within the last ten years and were released by no proper authority must . . . be sent back to work out their sentences. But if the men are elderly and have sentences dating back farther than ten years, they can be employed cleaning public baths and sewers, or repairing streets and highways.

SOURCE 25

a) Pliny to Trajan:

The citizens of Nicomedia . . . have spent 3,318,000 sesterces on an aqueduct which they abandoned . . . and demolished. Then they made a grant of 200,000 sesterces towards another one, but this too was abandoned.

I have been . . . to look at the spring which could supply the water to be brought along an aqueduct . . . There are very few arches still standing, but others could be built out of the blocks of stone taken from the earlier construction, and I think some ought to be made of brick, which would be easier and cheaper.

The first essential is for you to send out an engineer or an architect to prevent a third failure.

b) Trajan to Pliny:

Steps must be taken to provide Nicomedia with a water supply . . . But for goodness' sake apply yourself no less to finding out whose fault it is that Nicomedia has wasted so much money . . . It may be that people have profited by this starting and abandoning of aqueducts. Let me know the result of your inquiry.

Pliny and Trajan, *Letters*, written AD 111–113

activity

1 Look at source 23. Pliny had a problem about how to guard prisoners.
a What possible solutions to his problem did he have?
b What does Trajan's decision tell you about what he thought was most important?
2 Look at source 24.
a What most concerns Trajan about this situation?
b Does he come to a fair decision?
3 Look at source 25.
a What is Pliny most concerned about in his letter?
b What most worries Trajan about Pliny's report?
4 Look at sources 23, 24 and 25. Work with a partner to:
a Decide whether you think that the decisions of Pliny and Trajan in each case were fair or unfair, harsh or lenient. Maybe you can find other words to describe them.
b Make a list of everything these letters tell you about how the Romans governed the Empire.

assignments

I Here is part of a speech made by a Greek on a visit to Rome:

SOURCE 26

Now indeed it is possible for Greek or non-Greek to travel wherever he will, easily . . . it is enough to be a Roman citizen. The poet Homer said, 'Earth common to all', and you have made it come true. You have measured the land of the entire civilised world. You have bridged the rivers . . . and cut highways through the mountains . . . You have made all areas used to a settled and orderly way of life.

Aelius Aristedes, *In Praise of Rome*, delivered in AD 144

a (i) List all the benefits of living in the Roman Empire which Aristedes mentions. (ii) What other benefits can you think of?
b Write what you think Aristedes might have said in the rest of his speech if he had included all the points you have thought of. Go into as much detail as you can about each point, but try to keep to his style.
c What do you think were some of the disadvantages of living in a province in the Empire? Give reasons for your suggestions.

2 Choose any two from the following list and explain in detail the ways in which they helped to keep the Roman Empire together:
● the Emperor   ● roads   ● frontiers
● the army   ● trade   ● governors of provinces.

3 In this story set in the 2nd century AD a centurion is marching his men to go on guard in the fort in Roman Exeter:

SOURCE 27

The British town was spread below . . . a sprawling huddle of reed-thatched roofs . . . with the squared, clean lines of the Roman forum and basilica looking oddly rootless in their midst.

The road led straight through the town . . . Dogs sat scratching in odd corners, lean pigs rooted among the garbage piles, and women with bracelets of gold or copper on very white arms sat in hut doorways, spinning or grinding corn . . .

One day there would be straight streets, he supposed, and temples and bath-houses and a Roman way of life. But as yet it was a place where two worlds met without mingling [mixing] . . .

Rosemary Sutcliff, *Eagle of the Ninth*, 1954

a Using Parts 1–5, make a list of everything in the extract that is based on (i) historical evidence (ii) the writer's imagination.
b Do you agree with the picture the writer has created of a Roman frontier town? Give your reasons.
c Use historical evidence and your own imagination to try to bring alive an event or scene from the point of view of someone living in the Roman Empire. For example: a visit to the baths; watching a triumph; a shopping trip; building an aqueduct.

6

The Empire Becomes Christian

A cross and altar found in Herculaneum.

We can be fairly sure there were some Christians in Pompeii and Herculaneum when Vesuvius erupted because archaeologists found a cross and altar in a house in Herculaneum (source 1).

It was not safe to be a Christian in AD 79, even though the Romans were used to people who worshipped other gods. The Christians believed their God was the only true one. They could not agree to worship the gods of Rome too.

This made Christians seem disloyal, so in AD 64 the Emperor ordered Christians to be arrested. The Christian who put the cross up in Herculaneum had to keep his religion secret. He built a cupboard to hide the cross and disguised the altar as a chest.

Yet just over 200 years later, in 313, the Emperor Constantine announced that everyone, including Christians, could worship whichever gods they liked and Constantine himself was **baptized** a Christian on his deathbed in 337. In 392 the Emperor Theodosius banned all religions except Christianity. Christianity had become the official religion of the Roman Empire.

> **i** **Baptize** The act of making someone a member of the Christian Church. In the ceremony the priest pours or sprinkles water on the person as a sign that they are starting a new life as a Christian

This was a big change. Why did it happen?

Before you start to find out, remember that Christianity was a forbidden religion for more than 200 years before the time of Constantine. That means the change took a long time to happen.

Some of the causes of the change went back a very long time too. We call causes like that the <u>long-term</u> causes. They are the ones that make an event possible, but do not actually set it off.

You will find other causes that happened much nearer to the year 392 itself. We call these the <u>immediate</u> or <u>short-term</u> causes. They are the ones that set an event off. But they would not be likely to do so if the long-term causes were not already there.

The Christians

The Christians believed in the life and teaching of Jesus **Christ** who in about AD 26, left his home in Israel, the land of the Jews and the Roman province of Judea, to travel through the country and preach.

The Jews hated the Romans. They believed that a Messiah, or Saviour, would come and help them to drive out the Romans and once again make Israel rich and prosperous. When they heard Jesus, some Jews decided that the Messiah had come at last.

The chief priests of the Jewish religion did not like his message. He preached that God loved ordinary people however poor and humble, not just wealthy and powerful people. They told the Romans Jesus was dangerous and might lead a rebellion and asked Pontius Pilate, the Roman governor of Judea, to have him executed.

> **i** **Christ**   The name 'Christ' comes from the Latin word 'Christus' meaning 'anointed one' or 'messiah'.

The spread of Christianity

Jesus's followers believed he came back to life three days after his execution and that they saw him go to Heaven surrounded by a bright light. They believed that Jesus had died to save the world from evil and that people who became Christians and were truly sorry for the things they had done wrong would also overcome death by living a new life in Heaven. They started to travel outside Judea to·try to convert people living in other parts of the Empire.

SOURCE 2

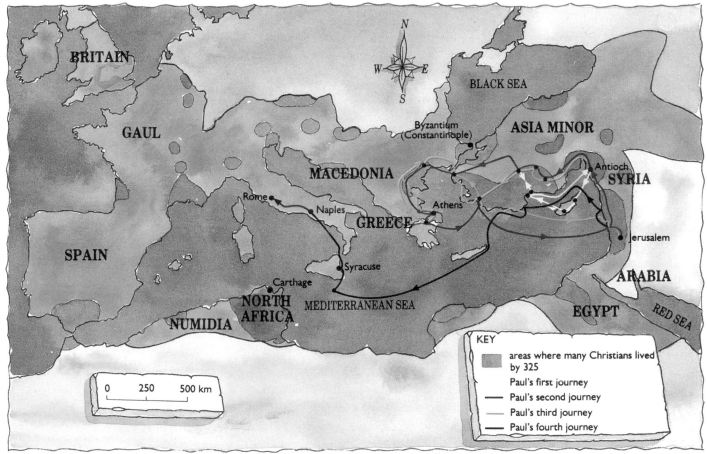

Paul's missionary journeys, and the spread of Christianity.

The one who did the most to spread Christianity was Paul, a tentmaker from the town of Tarsus who made four long journeys (source 2). He could speak and write Greek – the main language of people living in the east of the Empire. He taught that anyone who believed in Jesus – rich or poor, free or slave – could become a Christian.

Wherever they travelled, missionaries like Paul set up 'churches'. A church was not a building. It was the name given to several congregations, or groups, of Christians, who met in each other's houses. A church was always based in a Roman city and its surrounding countryside. A bishop looked after each church. All the churches together were called the Church. As the Church grew, Alexandria in Egypt, Carthage in North Africa and Rome itself became the headquarters for the churches in their areas.

The bishop of Rome was the most senior and, in the end, became head of the whole Church. This was partly because he was the successor of St Peter, the first bishop of Rome and the man Jesus himself appointed to lead his followers, and partly because of Rome's importance as chief city of the Empire. The first bishops were called 'papa' – father. Later that title was given only to the Bishop of Rome who became known as the 'Pope'.

> **i** **Eucharist**   At the Eucharist Christians followed Jesus's instructions and repeated his actions at the Last Supper when he ate bread and drank wine with his chief followers, the disciples. According to St Luke he said, 'This is my body, which I am giving for you, break the bread in memory of me', and 'This wine represents . . . my blood which is shed for you'.

The persecution of the Christians

Although the Roman government usually allowed people to follow their own religious beliefs, it soon began to turn against the Christians because they seemed to be a threat.

It was bad enough that they said their God was the only true God and refused to make sacrifices to the Roman gods and the Emperor; they also went around trying to persuade everyone else of their point of view. They tried to convert people.

Also, they met in private houses which made the Romans think that they might be plotting against the government. And they said that everyone was equal in the sight of God. That worried the Romans because they thought it would give slaves a reason to argue with their masters.

In addition most Romans misunderstood what the Christians believed. The Christians said people should love one another as God loved them. The Romans thought they meant people should have free sexual relationships. They thought this was immoral. When they heard that the Christians talked about eating Christ's 'body' and 'blood' at their act of worship, called the '**Eucharist**', they decided they must be cannibals.

The Christians were unpopular and the Romans started to hunt them down. The first persecution came in AD 64 when the Emperor Nero decided to blame the Christians for starting a great fire which burnt down over half of the city of Rome. Some people said he had started the fire himself:

SOURCE 3

> *In order to put an end to the gossip and suspicions, he laid the blame at the door of a group who were already hated for their evil practices – the Christians . . . Christians were arrested . . . All of them were charged but not so much because they were responsible for the fire, but because of their anti-social behaviour.*
>
> *Their executions were made laughable: they were covered in animal skins and torn to death by dogs, or were nailed to crosses and set alight when evening came.*

Tacitus, *The Annals of Imperial Rome*, completed early second century AD

Christians were forced to meet secretly. They even had a secret sign, the fish (source 4).

SOURCE 4

The Christians' secret sign. If you take the first letter of each of the Greek words for 'Jesus Christ, Son of God, Saviour' you end up with IXTHUS – the Greek word for fish.

activity

1 Look at sources 1, 3, 5 and 6 and the information in the text.
a Make a list of all the reasons why the Romans persecuted Christians.
b What effect did persecution have on the Christians? Is that what the Romans wanted?
2 Look at source 2. How do you think the existence of the Roman Empire might have helped the spread of Christianity in the first century AD?
3 What do sources 1, 2, 4, 5 and the information in the text tell you about the strengths of the Christian Church in the early days?

When Pliny was governor of Bithynia and Pontus, he had to ask for the Emperor Trajan's advice about the Christians:

SOURCE 5

*I am not sure . . . whether a man who repents [says he is sorry] should be pardoned for ceasing to be a Christian or punished for having been one . . . I tortured two female slaves called **deaconesses**, but I found nothing but a wicked and evil superstition.*

Pliny, *Letter to Trajan*, written AD 111–113

Trajan replied:

SOURCE 6

The Christians are not to be hunted out. If they are charged and found guilty, they must be punished, but not if they prove repentance by worshipping our gods. Then they must be pardoned.

Trajan, *Letter to Pliny*, written AD 111–113

Even so, the Romans continued to persecute the Christians on-and-off for over 200 years. Thousands of them met their deaths by being made to fight wild animals in the Colosseum.

Deaconess A woman who was an assistant to a priest. Male assistants were called deacons. A deacon could go on to become a priest; but a deaconess could not.

SOURCE 7

This mosaic shows wild animals attacking people in an amphitheatre.

The mystery religions

Serapis. This head was found in London.

Long before Christianity started to spread, many Romans had been interested in other new religions. Like Christianity these came from the eastern part of the Empire and, also like Christianity, they invited people to have a personal relationship with a god or goddess who would help them lead better lives.

You had to make a definite decision to join one of these religions – you had to be converted – and then you had to take part in special initiation (joining) ceremonies. Once you were a member, you were allowed to take part in the 'mysteries' – the secret ceremonies known only to true followers. That is why they are sometimes called 'mystery' religions.

Isis and Serapis

SOURCE 9

The worship of Isis. This wall-painting at Herculaneum shows the morning service of opening the temple.

activity

1 Look at sources 8–10 and the information in the text.
a What evidence is there that by the third century AD Romans were looking for new religions?
b Make a list of the ways in which the mystery religions were different from the traditional Roman religion.
c Why do you think the mystery religions might have been so popular?
2 Make lists of **a** the similarities, and **b** the differences between Mithraism and Christianity.

The worship of Isis and Serapis came from Egypt. Isis was the chief Egyptian goddess and wife of the god Osiris. An Egyptian legend told how Osiris was killed by Set, god of the underworld, who cut his body into pieces and scattered them across the land. Isis searched for all the pieces and when she had found them was able to bring Osiris back to life.

In later times the new Osiris was called Serapis. The worship of Isis and Serapis spread to Italy in the first century BC, though it was officially banned until the Emperor Caligula (AD 37–41) agreed they could become gods of Rome.

Mithras

Mithras was a Persian sun-god who was said to be always fighting against the god of darkness and evil. Legend said that he killed a wild bull and from the blood of the bull came all life on earth.

Only men were allowed to worship Mithras. His followers were organised in ranks, according to seniority, and had to live by strict rules. The religion became popular with soldiers in the Roman army and by the third century AD it was so popular throughout the Empire that it nearly became the main Roman religion.

SOURCE 10

A reconstruction of the inside of the Temple of Mithras in London. Mithras was supposed to have killed the bull in a cave so temples like this were often underground. Some of the ranks for followers had animal names such as Raven or Lion.

activity

1 Imagine you are a Roman emperor in the third century AD. What problems do the changes in peoples' religious beliefs give you? Make a list of them.

> **i Winter Solstice** *As the days get shorter in winter, the sun sinks lower in the sky until it looks as if it is standing still. This moment is called the winter solstice from the Latin 'sol' [sun] 'stitium' [stands still].*

The Unconquered Sun

By the third century the Emperors themselves were showing a strong interest in another religion quite different from the old Roman one. This was the religion of 'Sol Invictus' – the Unconquered Sun – which also came from the East, this time from Syria.

The Romans had always had a god of the sun – Apollo. The difference was that the Unconquered Sun was not worshipped as one god among many. His followers said he was the supreme and only god.

This idea was beginning to appeal to the Emperors who needed to find a religion that would unite all the different peoples of the Empire. In 272 the Emperor Aurelian returned from wars in Syria and built a temple to the Sun. In 274 he ordered that the annual festival of the Unconquered Sun was to be held on the day of the **winter solstice**, 25 December.

SOURCE 11

The Unconquered Sun.

The Christian Emperors

The conversion of Constantine

When Constantine became Emperor in 306, he was a worshipper of the Unconquered Sun. No one is sure exactly how he became a Christian. He himself told the story that in 312 he had a vision just before a battle and ordered his soldiers to put a Christian symbol on their shields. He won the battle and in 313 allowed Christians to worship freely.

Later he became a Christian himself, though he was not baptised until 337. Constantine still allowed people to follow other religions as well as Christianity; but he saw himself as the protector of the Christian religion.

The end of paganism

Christians called people who did not believe in Christianity 'pagans' or 'heathens'. In 392 the Emperor Theodosius made Christianity the official religion of the Empire. He ordered all pagan temples to be closed. Everyone in the Empire had to go to Christian services.

SOURCE 12

A Roman mosaic of Jesus Christ shown as a Sun God.

activity

2a How is source 12 (i) similar, and (ii) different to source 11?
b Source 12 was made after AD 313. Why do you think the artist decided to show Jesus Christ as a Sun God?
3a Do you think it is true to say that by AD 300 it was certain that Christianity would eventually become the official religion of the Empire?
b Why do you think it was that Christianity was chosen instead of one of the other religions?

assignments

1a Use the information in Part 3 (pages 43–49), Part 5 (pages 68–69) and in Part 6 to make a list of all the changes in Roman religion that took place from the time of Augustus to the end of the fifth century AD.
b Say whether you think each change happened rapidly or gradually. Give your reasons.

2 Here are some possible causes of the change from Christianity being a forbidden religion to its becoming the official religion of the Empire:

- Christianity survived persecution
- The Christian Church was well organised
- People began to be dissatisfied with the old Roman religion
- People became more interested in the mystery religions
- The Emperors needed to unite the Empire
- The Emperor Constantine became a Christian

a (i) Take each cause and say how you think it helped the change to happen.
(ii) Add any other causes that you have thought of.
b (i) Put all the causes in the order in which you think they happened.
(ii) Say whether you think each cause was long-term or short-term.
c Which causes do you think were the most important and which the least important? Give your reasons.

7

The Fall of the Roman Empire

By the end of the fifth century the Roman Empire had been split into two halves, East and West, and the western half had vanished with its provinces occupied and ruled by various German tribes.

The Empire did not collapse suddenly. The process took place gradually over hundreds of years; and for most of that time the rulers and citizens of the Empire were confident they could deal with the problems facing them. It did not occur to them that the Empire could fall.

Early in the fifth century, in 410, Rome itself was besieged and captured by a tribe called the Visigoths. Even this did not mark the end of the Empire, but for people at the time it seemed like the end of the world. Shortly after hearing the news Jerome, the bishop of Jerusalem, was about to dictate to his secretary:

SOURCE 1

I was so distracted with the affairs of the western provinces, and especially with the catastrophe at Rome, that as I began to speak . . . I could not find the proper words. For long I kept silent, knowing that this was the time for tears.

Jerome, *Letters to Augustinus*, early fifth century

The fall of the Roman Empire was certainly a great event in the history of the world. Historians have tried to explain it and artists have drawn episodes from the story. In Part 7 you can follow the events and look at the way some artists have portrayed, or pictured, what happened, and decide for yourself if you agree with their interpretations.

SOURCE 2

A German tribesman on the Arch of Constantine in Rome. The statue was made in the time of Trajan, early in the second century AD.

Problems in the Empire

Defending the frontiers

From the end of the second century and throughout the third, the frontiers of the Empire came under attack at all points (source 3). The pressure was greatest along the rivers Danube and Rhine where German tribes – such as the Goths, Franks and Vandals – wanted to cross over with their cattle and sheep to settle inside the Empire on the lands further south, where it was warmer.

Since there was not enough land to go round, the Romans wanted to keep them out. With the frontiers under attack in so many places this meant finding extra soldiers for the army and more money to pay them.

They started to find this difficult because plagues swept through the western provinces killing thousands. So there were fewer people to pay taxes and farm the land to grow crops to feed the cities. Gradually farms were left deserted and merchants began to make less money.

For the first time, the Romans found that they did not have enough money to pay for the defence of their enormous Empire. So the Emperors started to allow some tribes to cross the frontier and to settle the land that had been deserted. In return, the newcomers agreed to defend the frontiers against the tribes that had moved up behind them.

Another threat to the frontiers came from the Persians who in 260 even managed to take the Emperor Valerian prisoner (source 4) in a battle near Edessa.

activity

1 Look at source 3.
a What new problems did the Emperors face along the frontiers in the third and fourth centuries?
b What made these problems particularly serious?

SOURCE 3

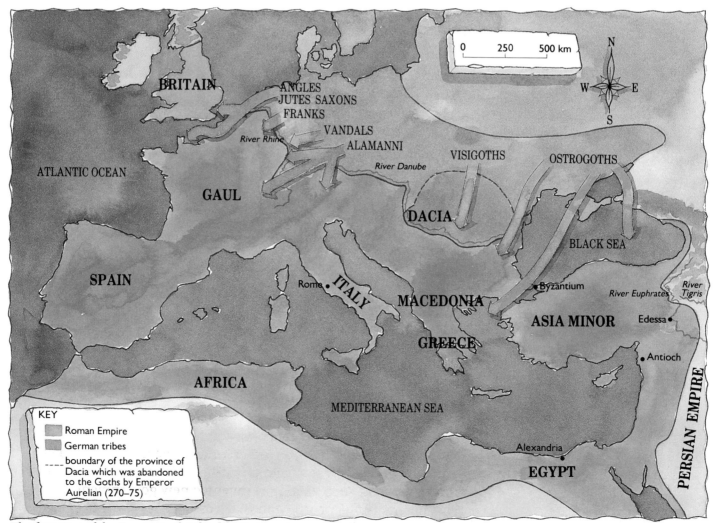

KEY
- Roman Empire
- German tribes
- ---- boundary of the province of Dacia which was abandoned to the Goths by Emperor Aurelian (270–75)

The frontiers of the Empire in the third century.

SOURCE 4

A rock-carving commemorating the victories of the Persian king, Sapor I, over the Romans. Sapor is shown holding the Emperor Valerian, captured in 260, by the wrist. His predecessor, the Emperor Philip, who was supposed to have surrendered to Sapor in 244, is shown kneeling.

activity

2 Imagine you are a Roman soldier who comes across the rock-carving shown in source 4 in the desert. What feelings might you have? Make a list of words that describe how you feel.

Weak Emperors

All these threats meant that it was impossible for the Emperor himself to deal with every crisis. So, the generals on the frontiers became more powerful. They often either challenged the existing Emperor or fought each other to decide who should be the next Emperor. The third century was a time of weak Emperors and civil wars. Between 211 and 284 there were twenty-three Emperors, each holding office for an average of less than three years. Twenty of them were murdered.

Recovery

The Emperors Diocletian (284–304) and Constantine (306–37) realised they faced new problems. First, the Emperors needed more money to pay the army. So they invented new government departments and appointed more officials to govern the provinces and make sure all the taxes were collected.

SOURCE 5

The head of a gigantic statue of Constantine made in about 313. The seated figure was over 9 metres high.

activity

I Compare source 5 with source 6 in Part 5. What has changed about the way the Romans portrayed the Emperor by the time of Constantine?

2a Work in pairs. Imagine you are Roman senators. You are arguing about Constantine's plan to move the capital of the Empire to the new city of Constantinople. One of you is in favour of it; the other is against. (i) Act out the argument. (ii) Discuss what you have both said with other pairs.

b Do you think all Romans agreed with Constantine's decision? Explain your reasons.

Second, the Emperors needed to be close to troublespots on the frontiers; but there were too many of them and they were too far apart. Diocletian's solution was to appoint a co-emperor, Maximian, who ruled in the West while Diocletian looked after the provinces in the East.

Constantine decided that Rome should no longer be the capital of the Roman Empire. He built a new capital at Byzantium, by the entrance to the Black Sea. He named it 'Constantinople'.

It was sensible to move the capital of the Empire to the East – the richest part of the Empire with good farms and great cities such as Antioch and Alexandria which traded with the merchants of Asia. It was also a good base from which to control the defence of both the Danube and Euphrates frontiers.

Despite all these changes, Constantine found he still had to allow many of the German tribes living along the Danube and the Rhine to cross the frontier and settle permanently in the Empire. This may have seemed like weakness on his part, but he turned it to the Empire's advantage by using the newcomers as officers and soldiers in the army. Soon the Romans used 'barbarus' as the ordinary Latin word for soldier.

As a result of the work of these two Emperors, the Empire in the mid-fourth century appeared to be as strong as ever. Yet once again it was about to be attacked by outsiders.

Invasion

SOURCE 6

At this time, as if trumpets were sounding the war-note throughout the whole Roman world, the most savage peoples raised themselves and poured across the nearest frontiers.

Ammianus Marcellinus, *History of the Roman Empire AD 96–378*, late fourth century

The reason for this new wave of invasions (source 6) was that the German tribes were trying to escape from a terrifying tribe from Asia called the Huns. The Huns were **nomads**, famous for their skill in fighting on horseback with bows and arrows.

Early in the fourth century the Hun tribes in central Asia started to look for better land on which to graze their flocks. In 367 they appeared in Europe. They over-ran the lands of the Ostrogoths ('bright Goths') and Alans, and moved on to attack the Visigoths ('wise Goths'). The Visigoths retreated to the River Danube and begged the Romans to let them take refuge in the Empire.

In 376 the Romans agreed to allow 100,000 of them across the frontier. There were thousands more behind them and the Romans could not hold them back. In any case the Germanic tribes were now in charge of frontier defence. The Romans were helpless.

SOURCE 7

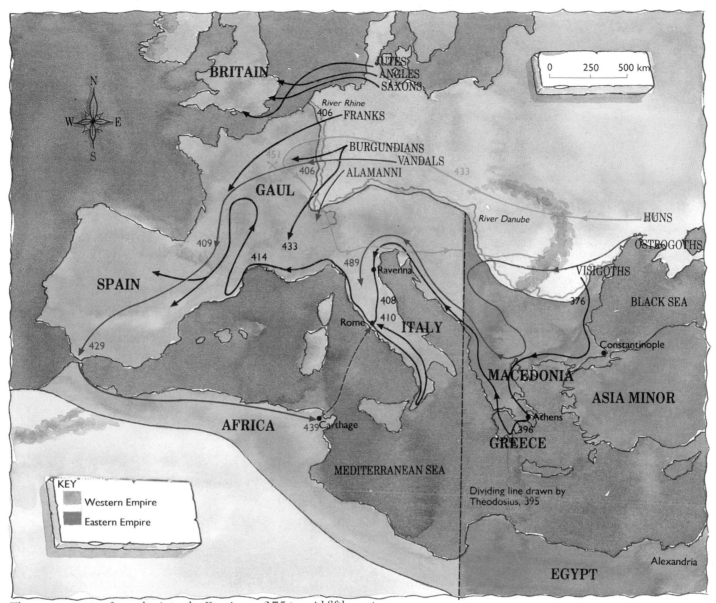

The movements of peoples into the Empire, c. 375 to mid fifth century.

i **Nomads** *People who do not have a fixed home, but move from place to place to find pasture for their animals.*

They tried to bargain with the invaders, but they failed and fighting broke out. The Visigoths destroyed a Roman army at Adrianople, and in 382 the Emperor Theodosius agreed they should live in the Empire under their own laws and rulers, in return for providing soldiers and farmers for the Romans.

When Theodosius died in 395 the Empire was permanently divided (source 7). Two Emperors took over – one for the East and one for the West. The one in the East ruled from Constantinople, and the one in the West from first Milan, then Ravenna – both in northern Italy and so closer than Rome to the threatened frontiers.

The end of the Empire in the west

Stilicho

When Theodosius died the Romans' agreement with the Visigoths broke down. Alaric, their ruler, claimed that money promised to them to buy food had not been paid. In 395 he invaded Greece and by 401 the tribe was in Italy, still demanding money and land.

They were defeated and turned back several times by Stilicho (source 8), the commander-in-chief of the Roman army, himself a

SOURCE 8

Stilicho with his wife and son.

barbarian – half-Roman, half-Vandal – and a skilful general. Each time Stilicho won, he was strong enough to destroy the Visigoths' army and end their threat altogether. But he allowed them to get away because he wanted Alaric to help him capture lands from the Eastern Empire.

> **i Gibbon** Edward Gibbon (1737–94) first had the idea of writing A History of the Decline and Fall of the Roman Empire when sitting among the ruins of ancient Rome while on a visit to the city in 1764. The six-volume book covers about thirteen centuries, from the time of the Emperor Trajan to the capture of Constantinople by the Turks in 1453.

The invasion of Gaul

On the last day of 406 came the greatest invasion of all. The Rhine froze over completely, allowing thousands of Franks and Burgundians to cross the river and occupy the whole of Gaul. One of the Empire's natural frontiers had at last given way. Looking back from the eighteenth century, the historian **Gibbon** wrote:

SOURCE 9

The . . . passage across the Rhine may be considered as the fall of the Roman Empire beyond the Alps . . . The barriers, which had so long separated the savage and civilised nations of the earth, were from that fatal moment levelled with the earth [flattened, removed].

Gibbon, *A History of the Decline and Fall of the Roman Empire*, completed 1787

The fall of Rome

Meanwhile, in Italy, the Emperor accused Stilicho of plotting with Alaric to put his own son on the Imperial throne. Stilicho gave himself up and was executed. Without him the Emperor could not deal with Alaric who now beseiged Rome itself, again demanding money and land.

Twice the Senate paid him to go away. The third time, in 410, traitors opened the gates and Rome was occupied by an enemy for the first time for nearly 800 years. Jerome heard the news in Jerusalem:

SOURCE 10

At the news my speech failed me and sobs choked the words I was dictating. She had been captured – the city by whom the whole world had once been taken captive. After that the brightest of earthly lights went out, when, truly, the very head of the Roman Empire was cut off, when, to speak yet more truly, the whole world perished along with a single city.

Jerome, Commentary to Ezechial, early fifth century

The Visigoths in Rome

The Visigoths stayed in Rome for three days. Then they first marched south, where Alaric died, and then into south-western Gaul where they finally settled. In 418 the Emperor accepted them as a people living in the Empire, but they kept their own laws.

Sources 11 and 12 are examples of how the capture of Rome by the Visigoths has often been seen since:

SOURCE 11

The Imperial city [Rome] was delivered to the ... fury of the tribes of Germany ... Alaric encouraged his troops ... to enrich themselves with ... spoils ... but he exhorted [encouraged] them ... to spare the lives of the unresisting citizens, and to respect the churches ...

Gibbon, *A History of the Decline and Fall of the Roman Empire*, completed 1787

SOURCE 12

The sack of Rome by the Goths, 410. A nineteenth-century engraving.

But there is evidence that after the Visigoths left, the city was still an impressive sight. Source 13 is some lines from a poem written by a Roman leaving Rome in 416 to return to his estates in Gaul which had been laid waste by the fighting there:

SOURCE 13

To number the lofty arches set with trophies would be a task like counting the stars, your glittering shrines dazzle the eyes ... Because you offered the conquered equal rights under your laws, you have made a city out of what was once a world ... It is time now ... to build on my ravaged estates, even if only cottages for shepherds.

Rutilius Namatianus, *On Returning Home*, written in 416

activity

1 What impression of the Visigoths and of the Sack of Rome does source 12 give?
2 How far does source 11 support this impression?
3 What evidence is there in source 13 that six years after the events of 410 Rome was still an impressive city?
4 The Visigoths were in Rome for three days. What kind of damage, and how much, do you think they probably did? Explain your reasons.

The Huns

In 451 the Visigoths joined with the Roman army and other German tribes to defeat the forces of Attila the Hun who had invaded Gaul. The reputation of the Huns was terrible. According to the historian Ammianus:

SOURCE 14

The people of the Huns exceed every degree of savagery . . . They all have compact, strong limbs and thick necks, and are monstrously ugly and mis-shapen. They eat roots of wild plants and the half-raw flesh of any kind of animal whatever . . .

Ammianus Marcellinus *History of the Roman Empire AD 96–375*, late fourth century

A Gothic historian, Jordanes, said of Attila:

SOURCE 15

He had the custom of fiercely rolling his eyes as if he wished to enjoy the terror which he inspired.

Jordanes, *History of the Goths*, mid-sixth century

Defeated in Gaul, the Huns turned to invade Italy instead. This time there was no army to meet them, but Pope Leo I set out from Rome to meet Attila and persuaded him to leave the country.

SOURCE 16

Pope Leo meeting Attila the Hun in 452. This sixteenth-century painting by **Raphael** is now in the Vatican, the Pope's palace in Rome.

---

i Raphael *Raphael Santi (1483–1520) was an Italian artist who admired Greek and Roman sculpture and used what he learnt from them in his own work. He produced many paintings for the Pope's palace, the Vatican.*

activity

5 Look at source 16.
a Raphael was not present at this meeting. So how useful do you think source 16 is as evidence for what happened in 452? Explain your reasons.
b What do you think Raphael wanted people to think about the Pope's meeting with Attila.
c Do you agree with Raphael's interpretation of this event? Explain your reasons.

The Vandals

Saved from the Huns, Rome then suffered at the hands of the Vandals who had captured Carthage (source 7) and with it the area of North Africa that supplied Rome with grain. From there they launched pirate attacks on Roman ships and in 455 they landed at Ostia and captured Rome itself. They stayed to loot the city for fourteen days (source 17) and then left with thousands of prisoners.

SOURCE 17

The Vandals sack Rome, 455. A nineteenth-century engraving.

SOURCE 18

A Vandal landowner setting out from his Roman villa in North Africa. A mosaic from late fifth- or early sixth-century Carthage.

activity

1 Look at source 17. What do you think the artist is saying about (i) Rome and the Romans, (ii) the Vandals?

2 Can source 18 be used as evidence to suggest that the Vandals adopted Roman ways?

3 What are the differences in the ways sources 17 and 18 portray the Vandals? Is anything the same?

The end of the Emperor

By now, power in the West was in the hands of the commander-in-chief of the army. In 476 this was a German called Odoacer who decided to ask the Emperor Romulus to grant his German troops the right to live under their own laws as the Visigoths did. When Romulus refused, the troops proclaimed Odoacer king.

Odoacer sent the Emperor into retirement and ruled Italy himself. From then on, the only Emperor was the one in the East.

SOURCE 19

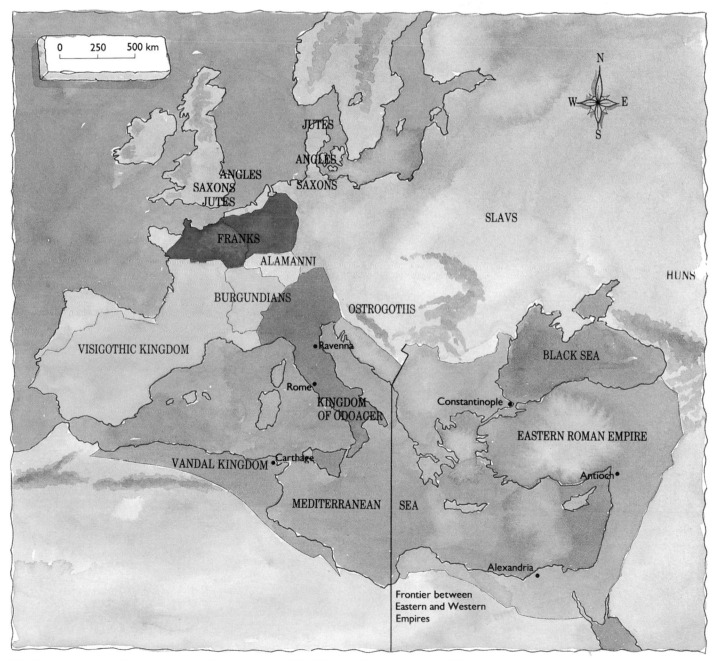

The Empire and the barbarian kingdoms after the fall of the western Empire in 476.

Viewpoints

It is difficult to say exactly when the Roman Empire collapsed. The process went on for a long time. Most historians see the moment in 476 when an Emperor ceased to rule in the West as the very end of the Empire. But, some point out that it probably made little difference at the time:

SOURCE 20

The 'end of the western Empire' was an event that no one at the time much noticed. There was no sudden collapse of Roman resistance against external barbarians. The barbarians had long been providing the army, and all that had happened was that the man with the real power assumed the ceremonial insignia [signs of office] as well.

Henry Chadwick, *On Taking Leave of Antiquity, The Roman World*, 1986

The story of the fall of something as big and powerful as the Roman Empire has fascinated historians for hundreds of years. Many of them have tried to work out why the Empire fell. Edward Gibbon managed to find more than twenty-four reasons. But in the end, he came to the conclusion that:

SOURCE 21

The decline of Rome was the natural and inevitable effect of immoderate [overmuch] greatness ... Instead of enquiring why the Roman Empire was destroyed, we should rather be surprised that it had subsisted [survived] so long.

Gibbon, *The History of the Decline and Fall of the Roman Empire*, completed 1787

SOURCE 22

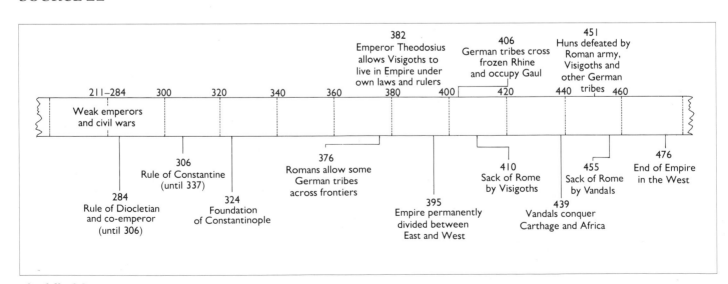

The fall of the Roman Empire

assignments

la Use sources I and 10 to make a list of all the things that you think Rome meant to Jerome.

b What else do you think Rome probably meant to him?

c Imagine Jerome kept a private diary of his thoughts and feelings. Write what you think he might have written in it on the day he heard about the Sack of Rome.

2 Towards the end of the first century AD the historian Tacitus wrote a book about Germany and the German tribes, partly based on his own travels. Here is some of what he said:

SOURCE 23

The power of their kings is not absolute . . . The chiefs debate matters of minor importance, but the whole community discuss major affairs . . .

It is well known that they never live in cities . . . They live [in villages] dotted here and there . . . They do not make use of . . . stone . . . or tiles; they use wood for everything . . . All wear a short cloak, fastened with a brooch, or failing that, a thorn . . . They also wear the skins of wild animals . . . The women dress like the men, except that some wear underclothes of linen, embroidered with purple . . .

It is a sin to turn anyone away from your door . . . Friends and strangers have an equal right to hospitality . . . They seldom beat or imprison a slave; but they often put one to death . . . in a fit of passion, as they might an enemy . . .

Tacitus, *Germany*, written AD 98

a Look at source 23

(i) Make a list of all the differences between the German tribes and the Romans. Were there any similarities?

(ii) The Romans described the German tribes as 'uncivilised'. What do you think they meant by that?

(iii) Do you agree? Explain your reasons.

b This is how one dictionary explains the meaning of the modern English word 'vandal': 'One who acts like a Vandal; a wilful or ignorant destroyer of anything beautiful . . . or worthy of preservation'. Look at the sources and information on page 98.

(i) How do you think the word came to have this meaning?

(ii) Do you think Vandals deserve to be remembered in this way? Explain your reasons.

c The same dictionary says that the word 'visigoth' can mean 'an uncivilised or barbarous person'. Look at the sources and information on pages 94–96.

(i) How do you think the word came to have this meaning?

(ii) Do you think Visigoths deserve to be remembered in this way? Explain your reasons.

(When you read about the Gothic kingdoms in Part 8, see if the sources and information there change or confirm what you have decided.)

3 In Part 5 you found out about the Roman Empire in the first and early second centuries AD. In Part 7 you have looked at it in the third, fourth, and fifth centuries AD. Use the sources and information in Parts 5 and 7.

a Copy down these headings: the Emperor and government; the army; the frontiers; wealth and trade. Now take each heading in turn and make lists of the ways in which things were different in AD 400 from how they had been in AD 100.

b Imagine Caius Pliny (pages 76–77) had been able to travel forward in time and found himself in the fourth century. Write the letter he might have sent to the Emperor Trajan on his return telling him about his experiences, thoughts and feelings.

4 Here are some possible reasons for the fall of the Roman Empire:

- The Empire was attacked from outside
- Events happened outside the Empire that caused new attacks on it
- The Romans made some decisions that turned out to be mistakes
- The Romans were no longer so prosperous
- Events happened which were completely beyond Roman control
- The Romans were not united

a Look through the sources and information in Part 7. Find examples of each of these causes. What other causes can you find?

b Take your list of reasons why the Empire fell. Decide which reasons were <u>most important</u> and which were <u>less important</u>.

c Look at source 21. Do you agree with Gibbon? Explain your reasons.

8
The Legacy of the Empire

In the end the Roman Empire collapsed; but that did not mean that everything to do with it either stopped or disappeared. Something left behind for other people when a person goes away or dies, is called a 'legacy'. That is why Part 8 is called 'The Legacy of the Empire'. It is about the things the Roman Empire left behind, some of which are still with us today.

Political legacy

The Gothic kingdoms

SOURCE 1

The Empire and barbarian kingdoms in 526.

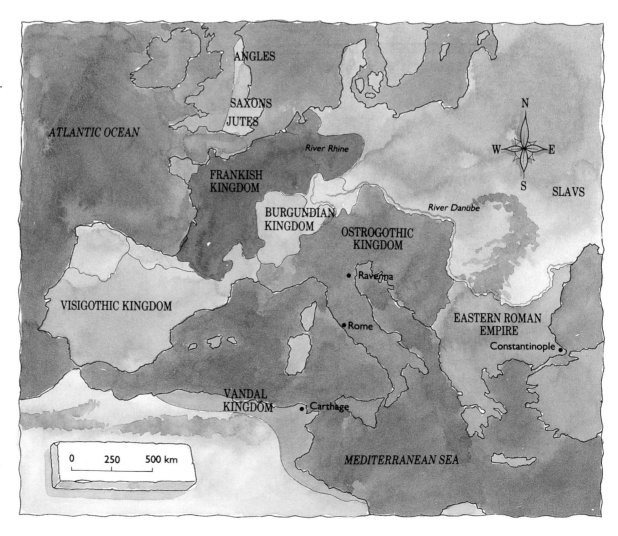

SOURCE 2

The palace at Ravenna of Theoderic the Ostrogoth who succeeded Odoacer in 493 and ruled until 526. This mosaic is in the church of St Apollinare Nuovo in Ravenna, which Theoderic built as his palace church.

In 493 Theoderic leader of the Ostrogoths deposed Odoacer and took over as king of a large Ostrogothic kingdom (source 1). Roman senators and landowners continued to live both there and in the kingdom of the Visigoths in Spain. They complained that the Goths wore trousers and greased their hair, but they also carried on trying to help in government and keeping alive Roman ways of doing things. Several Gothic kings drew up codes of laws which included Roman laws.

SOURCE 3

This gold crown was presented to a church in Toledo by Recceswinth, the Visigoth king of Spain, in the seventh century. It is decorated with precious stones. Recceswinth's name is written on the cross.

activity

I Look at sources 2 and 3.
a Make a list of all the information each source gives you about the Gothic kings.
b How does each source support the statement that some things to do with the Roman Empire continued under the rule of the Gothic kings?

The Byzantine Empire

SOURCE 4

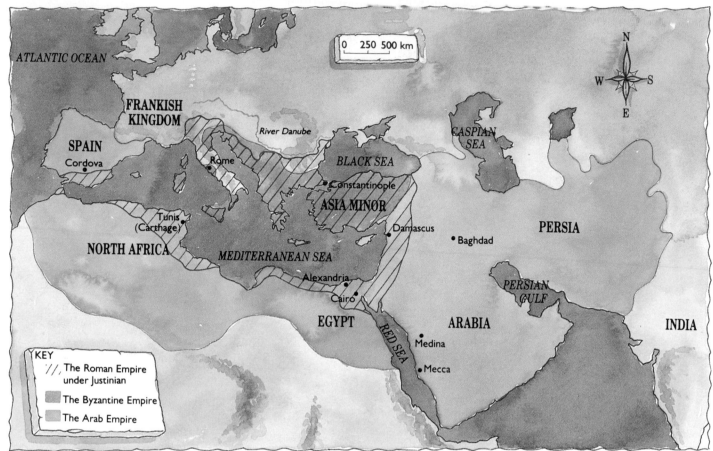

The Empire under Justinian (527–65) and the Byzantine and Arab Empires in about 730.

Justinian became Emperor in 527. His ambition was to win back the provinces of the Western Empire and re-unite them under his rule. He managed to re-capture many of those around the Mediterranean (source 4).

He is also remembered as a great builder (source 5) and because he ordered his lawyers to make a book bringing together all the old Roman laws. Lawyers still use it today.

Soon after Justinian's death in 565, the Lombards re-captured Italy. Less than a hundred years later, Arab armies had created their own vast Empire (source 4) in the name of the Prophet Mohammed and the new religion of Islam.

Once again the Roman Empire shrank. Greek rather than Latin had always been the language of the Eastern Empire and the Empire now became known as Byzantium, the name of the ancient Greek city which once stood on the site of Constantinople. Emperors continued to rule at Constantinople for nearly 900 years, but their links with the cities and countries in what had been the Western Empire grew gradually weaker.

activity

1 Look at sources 4 and 5 and the information in the text.

a Make a list of the ways in which the Roman Empire continued.

b Make a note by each item on the list to say for how long you think it continued.

SOURCE 5

The interior of the cathedral of Santa Sophia. Justinian had this built in Constantinople (now Istanbul) between 532 and 537. It has been a mosque since 1453 when a Muslim army captured the city. The concrete dome is 31 metres in diameter and 56 metres high. The first one collapsed in 558 and had to be replaced.

The Holy Roman Empire

SOURCE 6

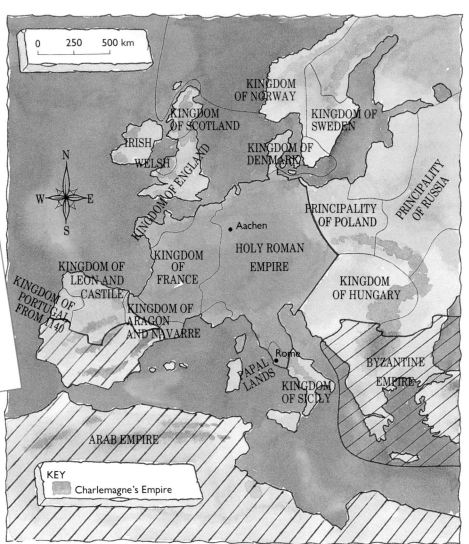

Charlemagne's Empire, and Europe and the Mediterranean region by 1100. By 1100 lands that had been in the Western Roman Empire were beginning to form into the kingdoms that became the basis for some of today's countries.

activity

I Look at source 6 and the information on this page.
a Do you think it was accurate to call the lands of (i) Charlemagne, and (ii) the Holy Roman Emperor an 'empire'?
Explain your reasons.
b Take the three words 'Holy', 'Roman' and 'Emperor' and say why you think (i) the Pope, and (ii) Otto I wanted each of them in Otto's new title.

The idea of a Roman Empire in the West went on long after the Empire itself had gone. In 768 Charlemagne became king of the Franks and extended their already large territories even further (source 6). As a reward for driving a tribe called the Lombards away from Rome, Pope Leo III crowned Charlemagne 'Roman Emperor' in St Peter's Cathedral in Rome on Christmas Day, 800.

When Charlemagne died, his Empire began to break up into smaller kingdoms. But, the Popes still needed a protector against their enemies. In 962 Pope John XII made Otto I, a Saxon king from Germany, 'Holy Roman Emperor' in return for his help. The Holy Roman Empire (source 6) was never very big, yet it lasted until the nineteenth century.

Religious legacy

By the time of the last Emperor in the West, Christianity had been the official religion of the Roman Empire for more than 100 years. Even though Rome was no longer the home of the Emperor, it was still the home of the Pope and therefore the chief city of the Church.

From the time of Constantine the Empire had protected Christianity and helped it to grow. When the Empire collapsed, its official religion did not. The Christian Church continued and Rome continued to be its headquarters. Even so, the tribes which had invaded the Empire were not Christian, nor were many citizens of the Empire who still secretly worshipped pagan gods.

Throughout the fifth and sixth centuries the Popes sent missionaries from Rome to convert people living in Ireland, Britain, France and Germany. As a result, Christianity eventually became the religion of the kingdoms of Europe as well as of the Byzantine Empire. The area where Christians lived became known as 'Christendom' (source 8).

activity

2 Look at sources 7–10 and the information of pages 107–8.
a What parts of the religious life of the Empire carried on after its fall?
b Did anything change and if so when?
c Which things to do with the Empire did the Church help to continue?

SOURCE 7

A recent photograph of Pope John Paul II giving his blessing from St Peter's Cathedral in Rome. The Pope in Rome is still the head of the world-wide Roman Catholic Church.

SOURCE 8

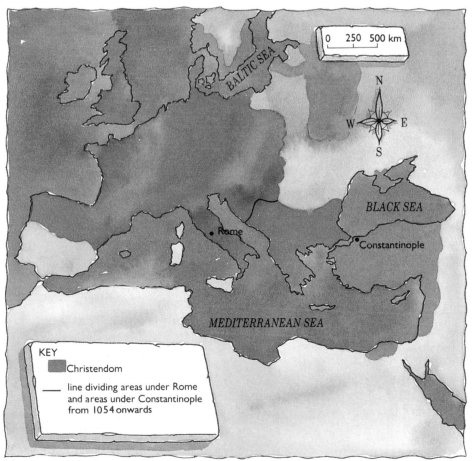

KEY

■ Christendom

— line dividing areas under Rome and areas under Constantinople from 1054 onwards

Christendom in 1054.

The Pope did not remain the head of all Christians. Even before the fall of the Western Empire there had been quarrels between the Popes in Rome and the Christians in the East. In 1054 the split became permanent when Christians of the Byzantine Empire formed their own separate Eastern Orthodox Church, with Greek as its main language.

In the West, priests and monks preserved the Latin language and made it the language of the Church (source 9). They also preserved a style of dress:

SOURCE 10

The clergy [priests] did not adopt [take up] barbarian dress at the time when their congregations were doing so, but continued to wear the 'Sunday best' of old Roman aristocrats [lords] – which we today think of as ecclesiastical vestments [church robes].

Henry Chadwick, *On Taking Leave of Antiquity, The Roman World*, 1986

SOURCE 9

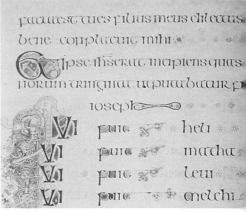

A page from the Book of Kells. This Gospel book was made in a monastery in Ireland or Britain sometime in the eighth century. The four Gospels are the part of the Bible that tell of the life of Christ. It is written in Latin and has painted pictures and decoration.

activity

1 How is source 9 evidence that, after the fall of the Empire, monasteries:
a helped to keep Latin alive?
b were centres of art and learning?

Ideas about government

Many people still admire the Romans for the way they managed to hold together and govern a large Empire that included many races, speaking many languages, and with different customs. In particular, the Romans passed on the idea that there should be clear laws which everyone must obey. The laws of many European countries today are based on the laws the Romans made and which Justinian ordered to be collected together and written down.

The Romans are also admired for the way they ran the Republic before the time of the Emperors. They invented a system of government which allowed the citizens to choose their rulers. It was also meant to prevent any one person or group of people having too much power. It did not always work and in the end they stopped using it, but many other countries since then have become republics and borrowed Roman ideas.

Some countries have borrowed Roman names, even if they do not describe exactly the same thing. For example, the United States of America, Ireland, France and Italy all have Senates; and the people who ran some areas of the British Empire in the nineteenth century were called 'proconsuls', a name the Romans gave to the governors of their provinces.

Cultural legacy

SOURCE 11

A page from a modern book on flowers

Language and literature

After the fall of the Western Empire, the Church, and especially monasteries, became the centre of learning and education. Because Latin was the language of the Church, it became the language which people who wanted to become educated had to learn to read and write. This was true until well into the sixteenth century.

Latin was used in law, science and medicine for much longer and still survives in these today. For example, doctors use Latin to describe diseases and parts of the body, and scientists use it to name plants (source 11) and animals.

In the sixteenth century it became popular for families to put a short Latin phrase or sentence, called a motto, on their coat of arms, or family badge. All sorts of organisations have Latin mottos today (source 12), including some schools and colleges.

SOURCE 12

The Royal Air Force emblem and Latin motto PER ARDUA AD ASTRA – 'Through adversity to the stars'.

> **i Shakespeare** *William Shakespeare (1564–1616), an English dramatist and poet, based his play* The Comedy of Errors *on one by Plautus. He based* Coriolanus, Julius Caesar *and* Anthony and Cleopatra *on the lives of Romans who he read about in the writings of the Greek author Plutarch (c. AD 46–120), translated into English in 1579.*

SOURCE 13

A scene from a Roman comedy. The actors wear masks. A slave brings home a drunken son whose angry father is waiting with a friend. This could be a scene from a play by the writer Plautus (254–184 BC). Sixteenth-century writers, including **Shakespeare**, learnt about Greek and Roman comedy from his plays and used the plots and ideas in their own.

Although from the sixteenth century onwards, most authors wrote academic books in their own language, Latin continued to be an important subject in schools. Even in the twentieth century most pupils in English secondary schools studied Latin until 1944. Latin also became the basis of languages such as Spanish, French and Italian, and many English words come from Latin.

Art and architecture

Italian artists first became interested in the art of ancient Greece and Rome in the second half of the thirteenth century. In the fifteenth century, architects and sculptors from Florence went to Rome to study the ancient ruins and sculptures. Interest in Greek and Roman art and architecture spread through Europe over the next hundred years.

Artists learnt from the realistic way in which Roman sculptors portrayed the human face and body, and often gave a statue a noble or heroic look.

Architects learnt from the way the Romans had used columns and arches, and also domes and curved ceilings, called vaults, which they often made out of concrete (source 5). Architects have continued to borrow Roman ideas and copy the look of their buildings ever since (sources 15 and 16).

SOURCE 14

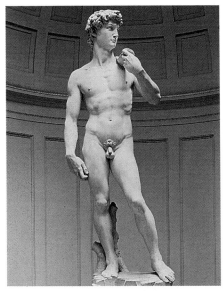

'David' by **Michelangelo**, 1501. Michelangelo carved this statue after his first visit to Rome in 1496.

> **i** **Michelangelo**
> *Michelangelo Buonarroti (1475–1564) was an Italian sculptor, painter, architect and poet. He worked in Florence, and Rome where he studied Greek and Roman sculpture.*

SOURCE 15

The town hall in Chesterfield. This was built in 1936.

SOURCE 16

The Arc de Triomphe, Paris, built between 1806 and 1836 to commemorate the victories of **Napoleon I**.

> **i** **Napoleon I**   *Napoleon Bonaparte (1769–1821) became the first Emperor of France in 1804 after the French Revolution (1789) had ended the rule of kings. Between 1805 and 1807 he conquered most of Europe. In the end he was overcome by an alliance of Prussia, Britain, Sweden and Austria and was sent into exile after his defeat at the battle of Waterloo, 1815.*

SOURCE 17

THE ROMANS ARE RUINING THE LANDSCAPE WITH ALL THESE MODERN BUILDINGS!

'The Romans are ruining the countryside with all theses modern buildings.' A cartoon of Asterix the Gaul, by Goscinny and Uderzo.

activity

2 Look at source 14 and source 19 in Part 3.
a What did Michaelangelo do that was similar to the Roman artist?
b What did he do that was different?

3 Look at sources 15 and 16.
a What ideas from Roman buildings did the architects of these buildings borrow?
b Why do you think each architect chose to borrow those ideas in particular?

assignments

1 What stopped when the Roman Empire fell and what carried on? Write an article or give a talk to explain your views.

2 The fall of the Roman Empire had many consequences.
a Make a list of what you think the consequences were under these three headings:

political (to do with the way people were governed);
religious (to do with what people believed);
cultural (to do with language, learning and art).

b Take each list in turn and decide whether each consequence on it was immediate, short-term or long-term.

3 It is often said that one of the most important legacies of the Romans was the ideas they had, and the example they set, about how to live and rule in a civilised way.
a Use what you have found out in this book to decide which ideas and actions of the Romans you think were (i) a good example to others (ii) a bad example. Explain your reasons.
b What lessons do you think we can learn from the Romans today?